easy

Microsoft® Outlook® 2000

See it done

Do it yourself

que®

MW01142950

Part 3: Tracking Appointments, Meetings, and Other Events

Part 4: Managing Your Contacts

Part 5: Keeping Track of Things to Do with the Tasks List

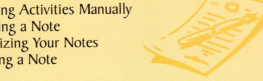

Copyright© 1999 by Que® Corporation

International Standard Book Number: 0-7897-1915-0

Library of Congress Catalog Card Number: 98-87894

Printed in the United States of America

First Printing: May 1999

00   99   98   4   3   2   1

Trademarks

Warning and Disclaimer

About the Author

Jennifer Fulton is a consultant, trainer, and best selling author of over 65 books covering many areas of computing, including DOS, Windows 3.1, Windows 95, and Windows 98. Jennifer is a self-taught veteran of computing which means, of course, that if something can happen to a computer user, it has probably happened to her at one time or another.

Jennifer began her writing career as a staff writer, before escaping to the life of a free-lance author, trainer, and consultant. She lives in Indianapolis with her husband, Scott, who is also a computer book author, and her daughter, Katerina, author-to-be. They live together in a small home filled with many books, some of which they have not actually written themselves.

Dedication

To my daughter, Katerina, who has changed my "outlook" on life.

Executive Editor
Mark Taber

Acquisitions Editor
Randi Roger

Development Editor
Brian-Kent Proffit

Managing Editor
Lisa Wilson

Project Editor
Rebecca Mounts

Copy Editor
Pat Kinyon

Indexer
Kevin Kent

Proofreader
Andy Beaster

Technical Editor
Brian-Kent Proffit

Interior Design
Jean Bisesi

Cover Designer
Anne Jones

Production Designers
Ayanna Lacey
Heather Hiatt Miller
Trina Wurst

Illustrations
Bruce Dean

How to Use This Book

It's as Easy as 1-2-3

Each part of this book is made up of a series of short, instructional lessons, designed to help you understand basic information that you need to get the most out of your computer hardware and software.

Click: Click the left mouse button once.

Double-click: Click the left mouse button twice in rapid succession.

Right-click: Click the right mouse button once.

Pointer Arrow: Highlights an item on the screen you need to point to or focus on in the step or task.

Selection: Highlights the area onscreen discussed in the step or task.

Click & Type: Click once where indicated and begin typing to enter your text or data.

1 Each step is fully illustrated to show you how it looks onscreen.

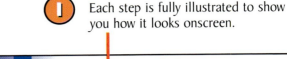

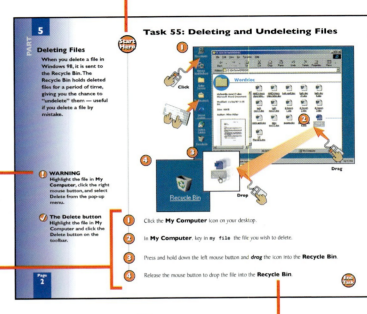

Tips and Warnings give you a heads-up for any extra information you may need while working through the task.

2 Each task includes a series of quick, easy steps designed to guide you through the procedure.

How to Drag: Point to the starting place or object. Hold down the mouse button (right or left per instructions), move the mouse to the new location, then release the button.

3 Items that you select or click in menus, dialog boxes, tabs, and windows are shown in **Bold**. Information you type is in a `special font`.

Next Step: If you see this symbol, it means the task you're working on continues on the next page.

End Task: Task is complete.

Introduction

Easy Microsoft Outlook 2000 is just what the name implies—the easiest way to learn Outlook 2000. What makes this book so easy to use? Well, just one look and you'll know: What you hold in your hands is the best step-by-step illustrated guide to Outlook 2000 on the market today.

If you're like most computer users, when you have to learn a new program such as Outlook 2000, you want to learn it in the easiest way. Like all of us, you don't have time to sit down and read an entire book just to figure out how to get your new program to work. You don't want to learn about every bell and whistle; you just want to know how to perform the most basic tasks. Good news, you've found the right book for the job!

Easy Microsoft Outlook 2000 presents you with the simplest, most visual way to learn how to use Outlook 2000—without rehashing the fundamentals. As a Windows user, you already know how to use a mouse, work with menus and dialog boxes, start and exit programs, and so on. You don't need to waste time reading about things you already know. Well, with this book, you won't have to. In fact, right now, you can skip to the exact task you want to perform and, without reading a thing, you can follow the easy to understand, visual steps that show you exactly how to accomplish that task.

So sit back, relax, and just follow the pictures. What could be easier? And in today's got-too-much-to-do kind of world, if it's not easy, why bother?

PART 1

Getting to Know Microsoft Outlook

Microsoft Outlook 2000 is an electronic day planner that enables you to keep track of important information such as appointments, meetings, contact names and phone numbers, email addresses, and the like. Outlook 2000 contains several tools (displayed as folders) with which you can organize your life:

- Outlook Today—A one page overview of today's appointments, meetings, things to do, and incoming email.

- Inbox—An electronic messaging system

- Calendar—An appointment and event tracker

- Contacts—An address book

- Tasks—An electronic to do list

- Journal—A business and/or personal diary

- Notes—An electronic post-it system

In addition, Outlook serves as a miniature version of Windows Explorer, providing complete access to your files—whether they're located on your computer, your company's network or intranet, or the Internet itself. Through Outlook, you can search for a file, open it, make changes, and even insert that file into an Outlook item, such as an email message, a Calendar entry, or the Journal.

In this part, you'll learn the basics of using Outlook: how to move between Outlook folders, how to sort each folder and change your view of it, how to access files through Outlook, and how to use Outlook Today.

Task 1

Task 1: Moving Between the Outlook Folders

Before you can use any of the Outlook tools, you must first switch to its folder. When you switch to a program, the actions menu changes to display commands specific to that tool. For example, when you change to the Tasks list, the Actions menu contains commands such as New Task and New Task Request. In addition, some of the buttons on the Standard toolbar are replaced with buttons you'd use only within the Task list.

Start Here

Click

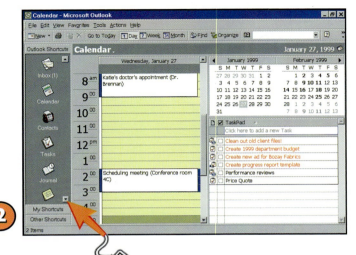

Click

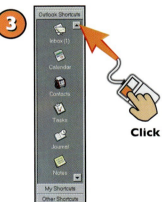

Click

✅ **Smaller Icons**
To display more icons at a time, right-click the *Outlook Bar* and select **Small Icons**.

✅ **Another Way to Go**
Want another way to switch between Outlook programs? Open the **View, Go to** menu and click the program to which you want to change.

1 To switch to a folder, click its icon in the Outlook Bar.

2 If you don't see the icon for the tool you want, click the **down arrow** on the Outlook Bar.

3 To redisplay the original set of icons, click the **up arrow** on the Outlook Bar.

Next Step

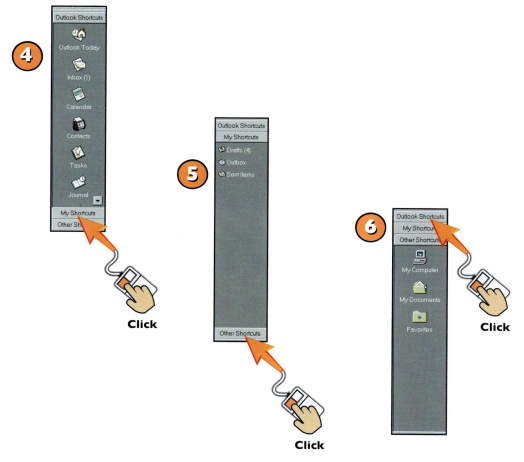

Use The Folder List
Another way to change to an Outlook folder is to select it from the Folder list. To display the Folder list, click the name of the current folder at the top of the window (for example, click **Inbox**). Then click the folder you want to switch to from the list that appears.

Where's the Command?
Only commands you use most often are displayed when you first open a menu. To view other commands, expand the menu by clicking the down arrow at the bottom of the menu.

(4) To access the Drafts, Outbox, or Sent Items folders, click the **My Shortcuts** button.

(5) To access a file on your computer, click the **Other Shortcuts** button instead.

(6) To redisplay the main set of icons, click the **Outlook Shortcuts** button.

Task 2: Using Outlook Today

Outlook Today presents a single page overview of the day's happenings. Here, you'll find appointments, meetings, and other events scheduled for the next few days. You'll also see the things you need to do and a summary of unread or unsent email messages.

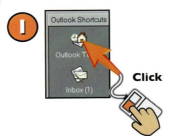

Click

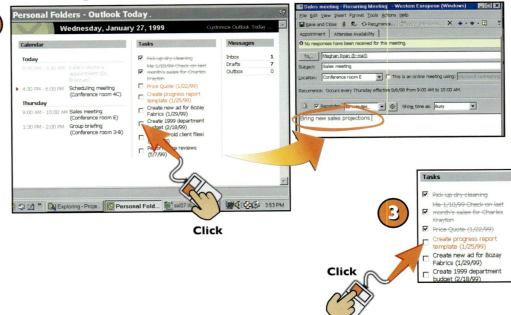

Click

Click

✅ **Great Way to Start Today!**
To display Outlook Today when you start Outlook, use the Options page. See Part 1, Task 3 for help.

✅ **What a Way to Go!**
To view the entire Calendar, Tasks list, or Inbox, click **Calendar**, **Tasks**, or **Messages**.

1 Click the **Outlook Today** icon.

2 To view the details of an appointment or task, click it.

3 When you finish a task, click its **check box** to mark it complete.

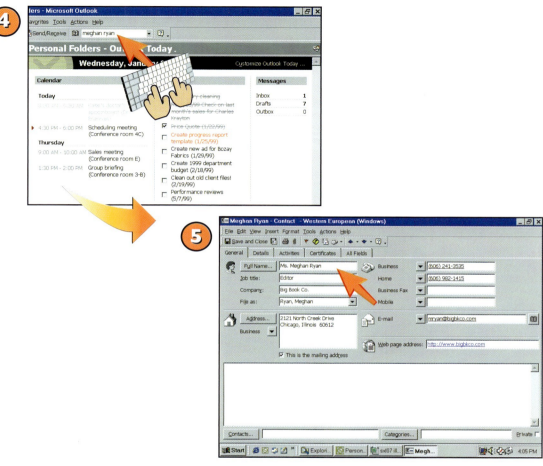

4 To locate information on a particular contact, type his or her name on the Standard toolbar.

5 To search for the contact, press **Enter**. The contact information appears.

Task 3: Customizing Outlook Today

Outlook Today helps you to quickly get a handle on how busy you're going to be today (and the next few days). So why not start your day with a cup of coffee and Outlook Today? You can customize Outlook to display the Today page first whenever you start it. You can make other changes to the display as well, as you'll learn in this task.

⚠ WARNING

If you don't want to change any options, don't click **Save Changes**. Instead, click **cancel**.

✓ Get Organized!

You can organize your incoming mail into various folders and have Outlook Today display the contents as well (or instead of) the Inbox, Drafts, and Outbox folders. See Part 7, Task 6 for help.

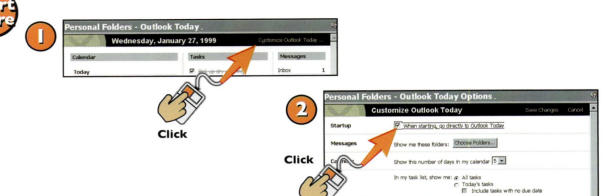

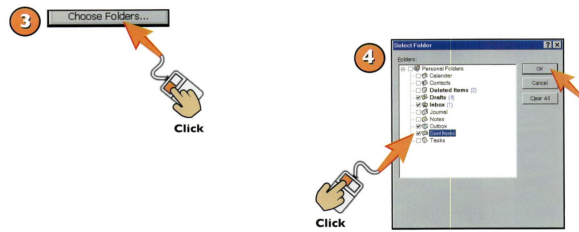

1 On the Outlook Today page, click **Customize Outlook Today**.

2 To display Outlook Today (instead of the Inbox) when starting Outlook, click **When starting, go directly to Outlook Today**.

3 To have Outlook Today check for email in folders other than the Inbox, Drafts, and Sent folders, click **Choose Folders**.

4 Click the folders you want to display, and click **OK**.

Click

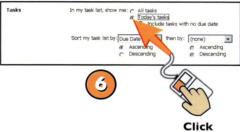

6 **Click**

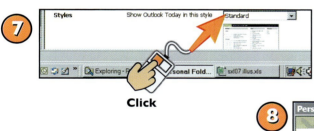

Click

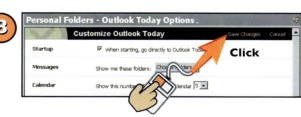

8 **Click**

5 To change the number of days for which appointments are displayed, select a number from the **Show this number of days in my calendar** drop-down list.

6 To display only tasks that are due today, select **Today's tasks**. If you want to include tasks that do not include a due date, select that option as well.

7 Select the style in which you want information displayed.

8 Click **Save changes**.

End Task

Page **9**

Task 4: Adjusting the Size of Columns

Information in Outlook is displayed in columns. For example, there's a column in the Inbox for the name of the person who sent the message, its *subject*, the date when the message was received, and so on. Sometimes the information in a column is not displayed completely because the column is too small. In this task, you'll learn how to adjust the size of your columns so you can see the information you need.

Start Here

1

2

Drag

3

Drop

✓ **Quick Fit**
To make a column the width of its longest item, just double-click the column's right-hand edge.

✓ **Resize It!**
You can resize other areas of the screen as well, such as the *preview pane* at the lower part of the Inbox. The various areas of the Calendar can also be resized, as well as the width of the Outlook Bar.

1 Move the mouse pointer over the right edge of the column you wish to adjust. The pointer changes to a vertical line, crossed by two arrows.

2 Drag the border to the right to make the column wider, or to the left to make the column smaller. A vertical line travels with the pointer to help you size the column.

3 Release the mouse button, and the column is resized.

End Task

Task 5: Sorting Items in a Folder

Start Here

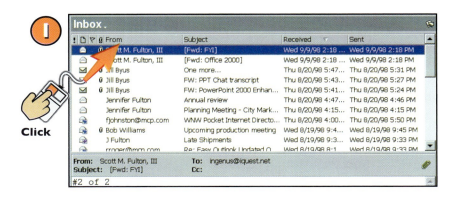

Click

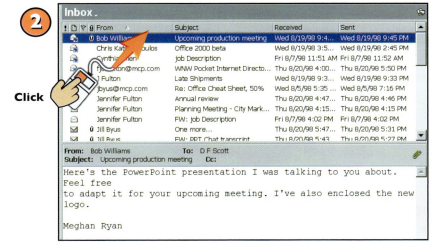

Click

Items in each Outlook folder are always sorted in a particular order. For example, the items in the Inbox are sorted by the date they are received, from the most recent email message to the oldest. You can reverse the order of how information is displayed, or you can change the column by which the information is sorted. For example, you can have your email messages sorted by the name of the *sender*.

✓ **What Sort?**
The column that's currently being used as the sort field is marked by an up or down arrow on the column's header.

✓ **Ascending or Descending?**
Ascending order arranges items from smallest to largest, or from A to Z. When ascending order is used, the column is marked with an up arrow. Descending is marked with a down arrow.

① To sort items by a different column, click that **column's heading** (title).

② To reverse the sort order, click the button marked by the **arrow**.

End Task

Task 6: Changing Views

Each of Outlook's programs displays its information in a particular way. To change the way in which information is displayed, change the view. For example, the items in the Contacts list are typically displayed as a phone list, with each person and his or her phone numbers shown on a separate line. You can display contact information in a card format instead by changing the view.

Start Here

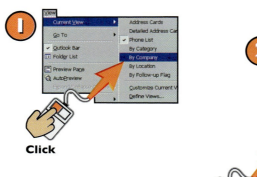

Click

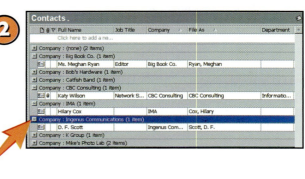

Click

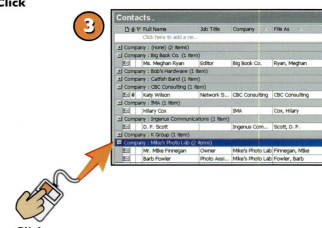

Click

✓ **Change the View**
If you select a view you don't like, simply select a different view.

⚠ **WARNING**
Some views actually *filter* out (hide) records that do not match certain criteria.

1 Open the **View** menu and select **Current View**, then select a view off the cascading menu.

2 If the view you select uses grouping, click the **plus sign** to view the items in a group.

3 To hide the items in a group, click the **minus sign**.

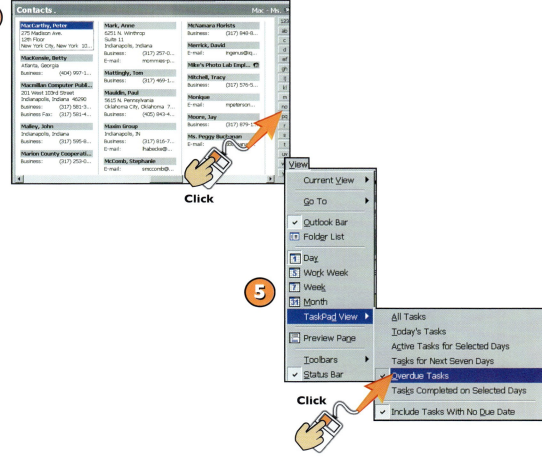

Click

Click

4 In contacts, you can select **Address Cards** view. To display a particular contact, click the button that matches the first letter in his or her last name.

5 In Calendar, you can select different viewing options for the calendar and the TaskPad.

Stand by Your Group
Some views group like items together, such as all the email messages sent by a particular person. To view the items in a group, click that group's **plus** sign. To hide the items in a group, click the **minus** sign that appears.

Outlook provides quick access to your documents, which you'll often find convenient. For example, suppose you're working on an email message and you want to include a copy of your sales worksheet, but you know that its figures are not current. No problem—just open the file, make your changes, and then insert the updated worksheet into an email message, *all without actually leaving Outlook!*

✓ Start Anew
You can also create a new Office document from within Outlook, as you'll learn in Part 1, Task 8.

✓ Recent Files in Your Journal
Access recently used Office files more quickly by using the Journal (see Part 6, Task 2).

✓ Can't Find a File?
If you can't locate your file, you can have Outlook search for it (see Part 7, Task 5).

Task 7: Opening a Document from Within Outlook

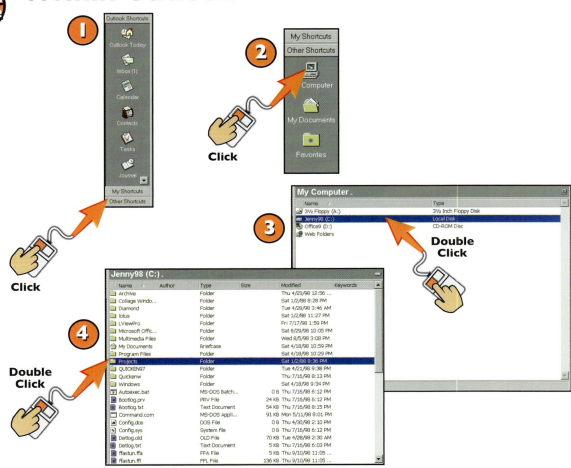

1 Click the **Other Shortcuts** button on the Outlook Bar.

2 Click **My Computer.** If you save your Office files in the My Documents or My Favorites folders (a common practice), click one of those icons instead.

3 Double-click a drive from the list.

4 Double-click a folder to display its files. Double-click subfolders as needed until the file you want is displayed.

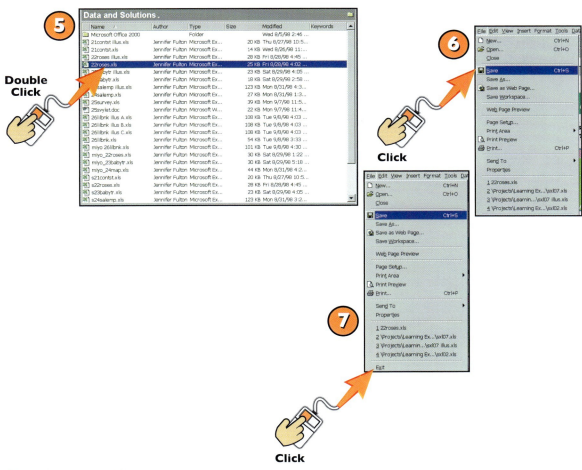

Double Click

Click

Click

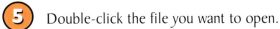
Double-click the file you want to open.

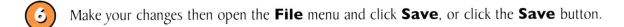
Make your changes then open the **File** menu and click **Save**, or click the **Save** button.

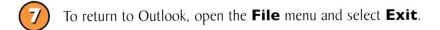
To return to Outlook, open the **File** menu and select **Exit**.

End Task

Task 8: Creating an Office Document from Outlook

Since hardly anyone works in a single program at a time, it makes sense that you can launch other programs and create documents with a few simple clicks from within Outlook. And after creating an Office document, such as a Word report or an Excel worksheet, you can include it with an Outlook email message or *link* it to an appointment, task, or contact name.

Click

Click

Click

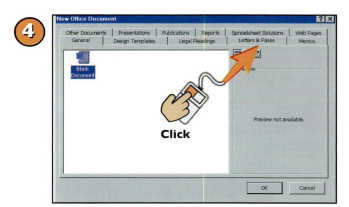

Click

✓ **What's a Template?**
A *template* is a semi-completed document of a particular type. Office provides numerous templates for common documents such as letters, expense reports, memos, and so on.

✓ **Post It!**
If you want to post (store) the new document in an Outlook folder, such as your Contacts folder, switch to that folder before you begin.

1 Click **Other Shortcuts**.

2 Click **My Documents**.

3 Click the arrow on the **New** button, and then select **Office Document.**

4 Click the tab that contains the template for the document you want to create.

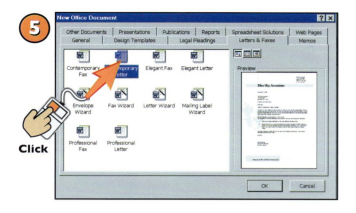

Click

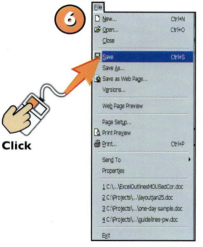

Click

Click

⑤ Click a template, and then click **OK**.

⑥ After completing your document, open the **File** menu and click **Save**, or click the **Save** button.

⑦ To return to Outlook, open the **File** menu and select **Exit**.

PART 2

Sending and Receiving Electronic Mail with Inbox

With the **Inbox**, you can send and receive electronic **messages**, or *email* for short. To send email messages, your computer must have a **modem** installed, and you must have access to a messaging service. A messaging service is like an electronic version of the Post Office. For a fee, you can "drop off" your messages, and the service will deliver them. The service will also accept messages for you that you can retrieve whenever it's convenient.

There are a lot of different messaging services to which you can belong, including the **Internet**, Microsoft Network, CompuServe, America Online, and Prodigy. All of these services provide more than simple message handling; choose the service that best suits your needs.

Tasks

Task 1: Creating and Sending a Message

Start Here

To send an *email* message to someone, you must enter an address. An Internet address might look like this: **jfulton@bigco. com.** The first part, jfulton, is the name by which that person is known on their *mail server* (the computer that handles their email). The second part, which follows the @ sign, is the domain name of the mail server. When entering an Internet address, be careful with upper and lower case; the address **joesnow@INDY. NET** is not the same as **joesnow@indy.net.**

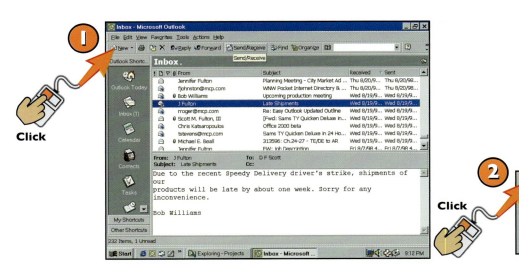

Click

Click

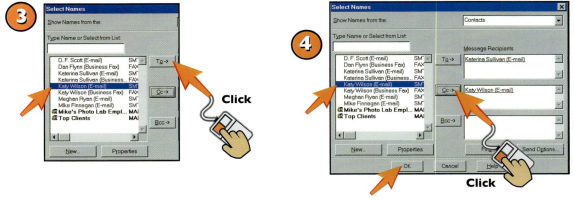

Click

Click

1 Click the **New Mail Message** button on the Standard toolbar. The Message window appears.

2 Click **To**.

3 Select a recipient, and then click **To**. Repeat to add more names.

4 Select a name and click **Cc** to send a copy of the message to someone. To send a blind copy, click **Bcc** instead. Click **OK**.

Next Step

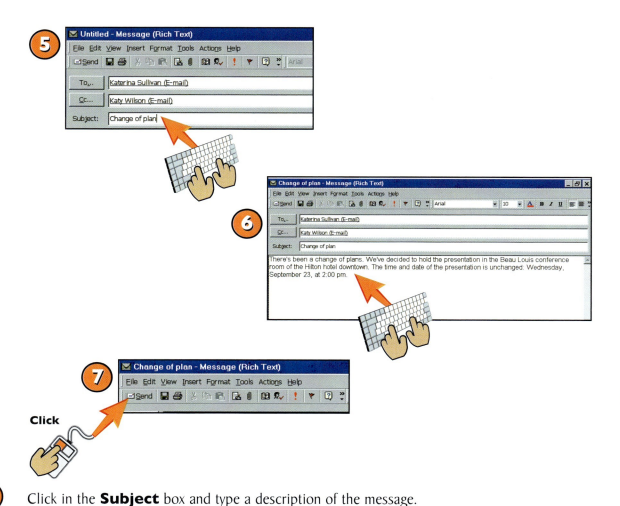

You compose an email message just as you might type a letter in **Word.** But unlike a conventional letter, an email message can contain other information in the form of files: a client database, a budget spreadsheet, or a sales chart (graph). See Part 2, Task 8 for help with attaching files to email messages.

Click

⑤ Click in the **Subject** box and type a description of the message.

⑥ Type your message in the large text box.

⑦ Click **Send**. A copy of the message is placed in the **Sent** folder.

⚠ WARNING
If your message was not sent right away, it was placed in the *Outbox* folder, awaiting delivery. This can happen if you select the *Remote Mail* or similar option when setting up your messaging service.

✓ Format That Text
You can add formatting to your message text; see Part 2, Tasks for help.

Task 2: Creating a Message Using Stationery

Outlook provides many different kinds of *stationery* (or templates) that you can use to create email messages. Each stationery has its own designer look— from stars, to flames, to bold lines and geometric shapes. Using stationery allows you to personalize your email message.

Start Here

Click

Click

Click

✅ **More Stationery?**
The first time you perform this task, you must select the stationery you want. Later, you'll find the name of that stationery on the New Mail Message Using menu.

Click

⚠️ **WARNING**
For your recipient to enjoy your stationery message, he or she must use an email program that supports *HTML* formatting, such as Outlook, Netscape Mail, or Windows Messaging.

① Open the **Actions** menu and select **New Mail Message Using**. Then select **More Stationery**.

② Select a stationery and click **OK**.

③ If the stationery you selected is not installed, click **Yes** to install it now.

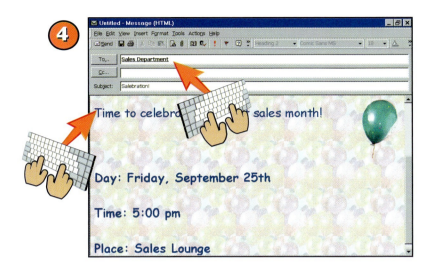

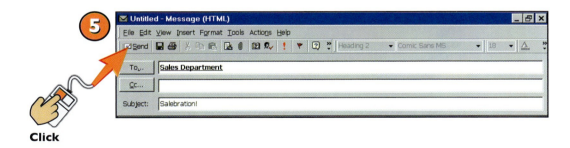

Click

④ Enter an address in the **To** box, type a **Subject**, and type your message.

⑤ Click **Send**.

✓ **Do You Use Word?**
If you use Word as your email editor, you can select from additional stationery options by clicking the **New Message** button, opening the **Format** menu, and selecting **Theme**.

✓ **More Stationery**
If you have a connection to the Internet, you can download more stationery from Microsoft's Web site by clicking **Get More Stationery** in Step 2.

End
Task

Task 3: Formatting Text

To add emphasis to the words in your message, you can format them. With formatting, you can add bold, italic, or underline. In addition, you can change the font (typestyle), size, color, or alignment of your text. You can even create bulleted lists (a list of items, each of which is preceded by a small bullet or dot), or numbered items.

Start Here

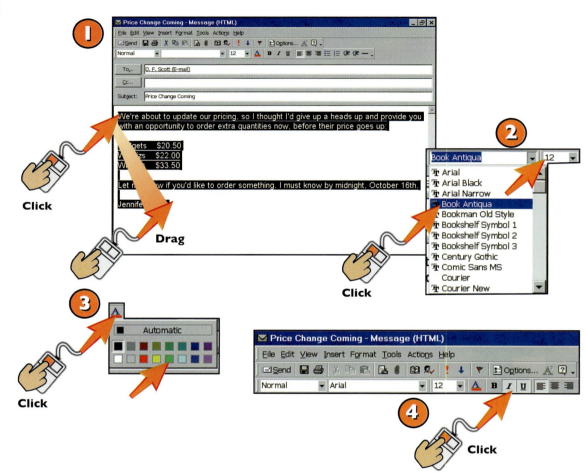

Click

Drag

Click

Click

Click

Click

✔ **Before or After?**
When applying formatting, you can change selected text, as shown in the steps, or you can turn formatting on and off as you type.

⚠ **WARNING**
These options are not available if you select a plain text message. In addition, some options are not available with Microsoft Outlook Rich Text, but only HTML.

1 Select the text you wish to change.

2 To change the typeface and size of text, select a font from the **Font** list, and a point size from the **Font Size** list.

3 To change the color of text, click the **Font Color** button, and select a color.

4 If you want, click the **Bold**, **Italic**, or **Underline** buttons.

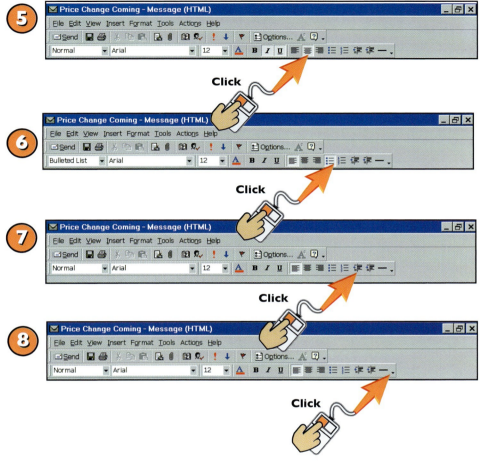

To add a horizontal line to a messsage, you must use HTML. This means you must either select this option off the **Actions, New Mail Message Using Menu**. You can also select a stationery, which puts you in HTML mode.

⑤ To change the alignment of text, click the **Align Left**, **Center**, or **Align Right** button.

⑥ If you want, click the **Bullets** or **Numbering** button.

⑦ To add an indent, click **Increase Indent**. To remove it, click **Decrease Indent**.

⑧ To add a horizontal line, click **Insert Horizontal Line**.

✅ **What a Combination!**
You can click more than one button to combine formats, such as bold and italic.

✅ **Pushed In**
When a format is turned on, the button looks "pushed in."

End Task

Task 4: Setting Message Options

Outlook allows you to set many message options, including the *importance* of a message (which helps the recipient identify which message to read first), and its sensitivity (which helps keep the message from others who may have access to the recipient's mail box). You can request a receipt—a return message telling you when the recipient has received and/or read your message. In addition, you can set a delivery date (which causes Outlook to hold the message in your Inbox for a while), and an expiration date (which notifies the recipient that the message contents have expired after a particular date and/or makes the message unavailable.) Lastly, you can select a *category* for the message to help you identify and organize the message later.

Start Here

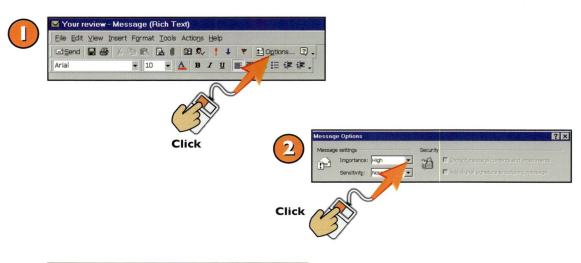

Click

Click

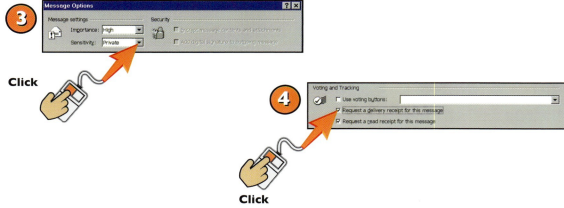

Click

Click

1. Click **Options**.

2. Select the **Importance** of the message.

3. Select the level of **Sensitivity** (**Normal**, **Private**, **Confidential**, and so on).

4. Choose a delivery and/or read receipt (a message that is sent back to you once your message has been delivered and/or read).

Next Step

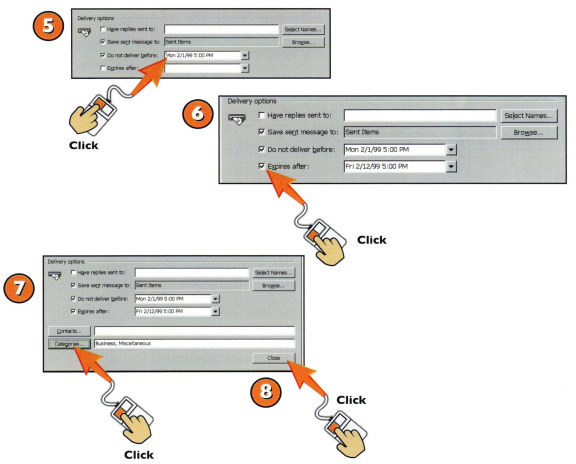

Click

Click

Click

Click

5 Set the date when you want the message delivered.

6 Set a date when you want the message to expire.

7 Select a category for this message.

8 Click **Close**.

End Task

Task 5: Specifying Where Replies to Your Messages are Sent

Normally, if someone opens a message from you and then replies to it, the *reply* is automatically addressed to you. In some cases, you may want a subordinate to receive the replies to a particular message instead. For example, if you've reassigned a project to someone else, you might want him to receive the replies to your project queries. You also can have replies sent to yourself (as normal) *in addition to another person or persons.*

✓ **One at a Time**
You can only direct the replies of this one message to someone else; not all messages.

✓ **An Alternative**
If you assign someone else to handle your email, he or she can read and respond to all your messages, including replies. See Part 2, Task 35.

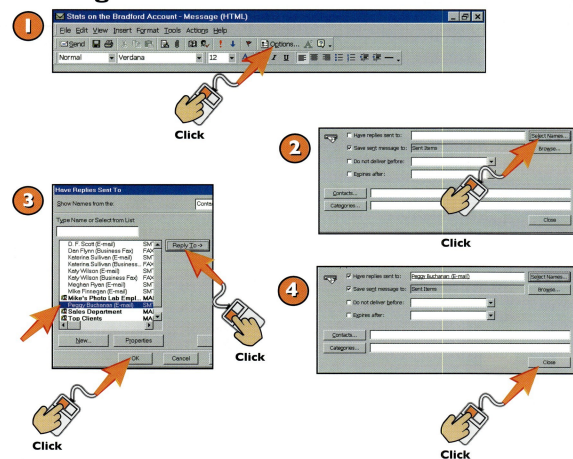

Start Here

Click

Click

Click

Click

Click

1 Click **Options**.

2 Click **Select Names**.

3 Click a name in the left list, and then click **Reply To**. Click **OK**.

4 Click **Close**.

End Task

Task 6: Saving a Message and Sending it Later

Start Here

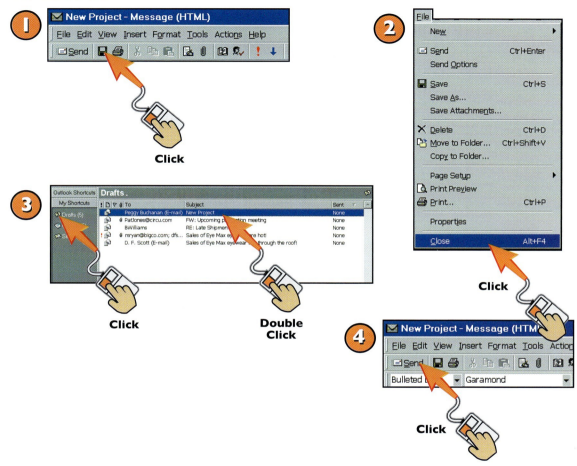

1 New Project - Message (HTML)

Click

2 File menu

Click

3 Drafts

Click — Double Click

4 New Project - Message (HTM

Click

If you're composing a message and you don't have all the facts you need just yet, you can save the message as a *draft* and send it later when you're ready.

① WARNING
Messages saved to the Drafts folder are kept there until you tell Outlook to send them.

✓ Ready to Go!
If you don't need to make changes to a draft message, you can send it immediately by right-clicking the message, selecting **Move to Folder**, and selecting **Outbox**.

1 Click **Save**.

2 Open the **File** menu and click **Close**.

3 To finish the message later, open the **Drafts folder**, and double-click the message to open it.

4 Make your changes and click **Send**.

End Task

Task 7: Recalling a Message You've Sent

After sending a message, you may remember some bit of information you forgot to add and may want to be able to recall that message and start over. No problem! Just recall the message, make the needed changes, and resend it.

Start Here

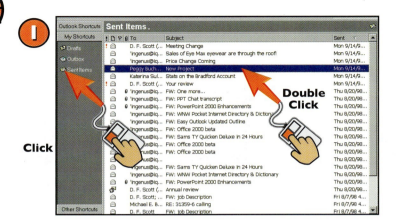

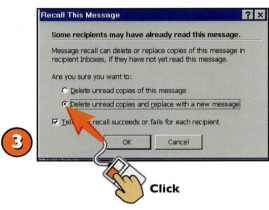

✔ **Leave it Alone**
You don't have to replace the original message after recalling it. Just select the **Delete unread copies of this message** option in step 3.

⚠ **WARNING**
There is a catch, however: you can only recall a message from someone who has not already read it. Also, the recall feature must be supported by his or her mail server.

1 Open the **Sent Items** folder, and double-click the message you want to recall.

2 Open the **Actions** menu and select **Recall This Message**.

3 Select **Delete unread copies and replace with a new message**.

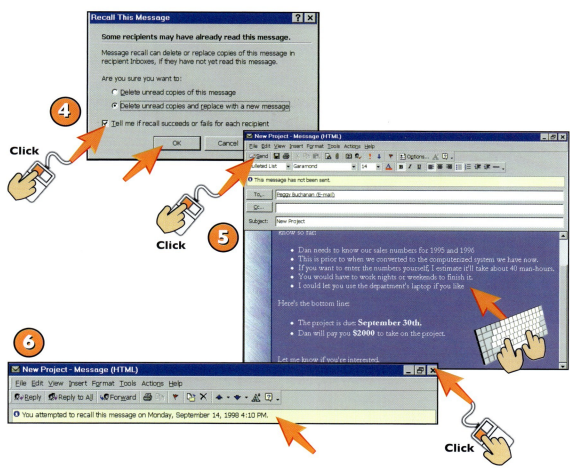

Click

Click

Click

4 Select **Tell me if recall succeeds or fails for each recipient** and then click **OK**.

5 Make changes to the original message as needed, and click **Send**.

6 You're returned to your original message. A note at the top of the window tells you that you have attempted to recall this message. Click the **Close** button.

! WARNING
The new message will only be sent if the old message was successfully recalled.

Task 8: Resending a Message

Sometimes you will want to resend a message (which is different than recalling a message and then possibly resending it—see Part 2, Task 7.) For example, if the recipient deleted the message accidentally, you can send him another copy.

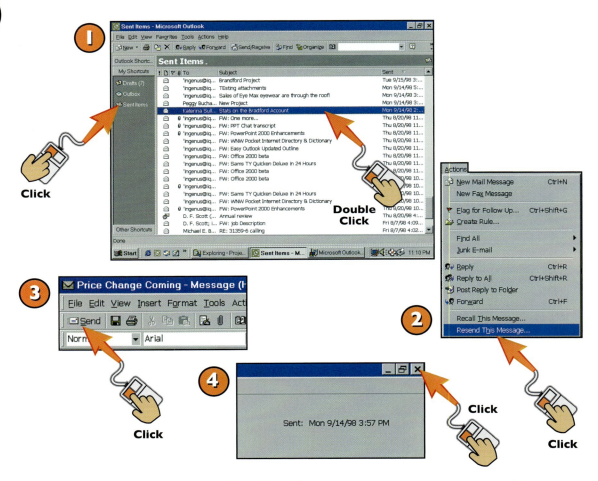

Start Here

Click

Double Click

Click

Click

Click

Click

✓ History Doesn't Have to Repeat Itself
You can make changes to the original message before resending it. You can even send it to additional people.

✓ Still There
You can resend any message that's still in your Sent folder. By the way, messages remain in the Sent folder until you delete them.

① Open the **Sent Items** folder and double-click on the message you want to resend.

② Open the **Actions** menu and select **Resend This Message**.

③ Click **Send** to resend the message.

④ The original message window appears. Click **Close**.

End Task

Task 9: Attaching a File to a Message

Start Here

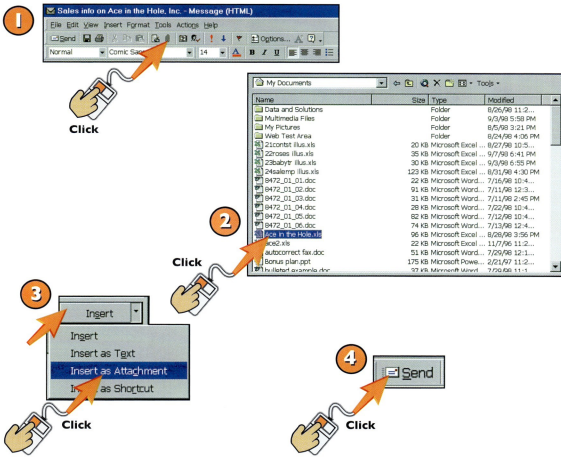

Click

Click

Insert
- Insert
- Insert as Text
- Insert as Attachment
- Insert as Shortcut

Click

Send

Click

If you *attach* a file, the actual file is sent with the message. To be able to open the file, the user must have a compatible program. If he doesn't have the proper program, you can send the file as *text*—in the body of the message itself. This assumes you can open the file and save it as text first. Lastly, you can insert a *hyperlink* or shortcut to the file. When the user clicks this hyperlink, the file is displayed. (See Part 2, Task 10 for help.)

✅ **Quick Way to Attach a File**
You can also attach a file by simply dragging it from Windows Explorer into an open message window.

⚠️ **WARNING**
Some files are rather large and take a long time to send and receive. Use a compression utility such as WinZip to make the files smaller before you send them.

1. Click **Insert File**.

2. Select the file you want to attach.

3. Click the arrow on the **Insert** button and select the option you want. (**Insert** and **Insert as Attachment** are the same.)

4. Click **Send** to send your message.

End Task

Task 10: Inserting a Hyperlink to a File

A *hyperlink* is a bit of underlined text that, when clicked, opens (displays) the associated file. You can insert your own hyperlink into a message and, when the recipient clicks it, he or she can then display the associated file. You might include a hyperlink rather than actually attaching the file itself, as discussed in Part 2, Task 9. You can add other hyperlinks as well; see Part 2, Task 1 for help.

⚠ WARNING

The recipient must have access to the file's location for this to work. In most cases, you will use this to share your files through a *network* or an *intranet*. However, you can include links to public files on the Internet as well. Also you must use an HTML message for this task.

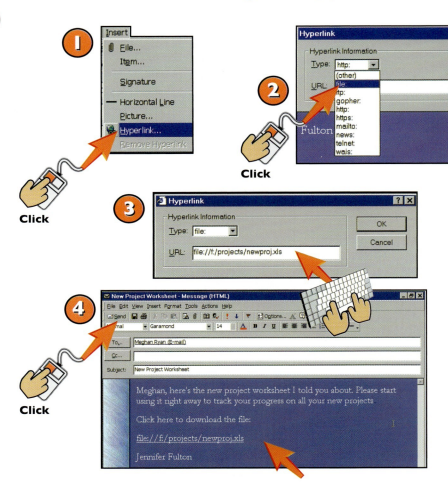

Start Here

Click

Click

Click

Click

① Open the **Insert** file and select **Hyperlink**.

② Select **file:** from the **Type** list.

③ Type the location of the file in the **URL** text box, like this:
`file://f:/projects/newproj.xls` and click **OK**.

④ The *link* appears as hypertext. Click **Send**.

End Task

Task 11: Adding a Link to a Web Page

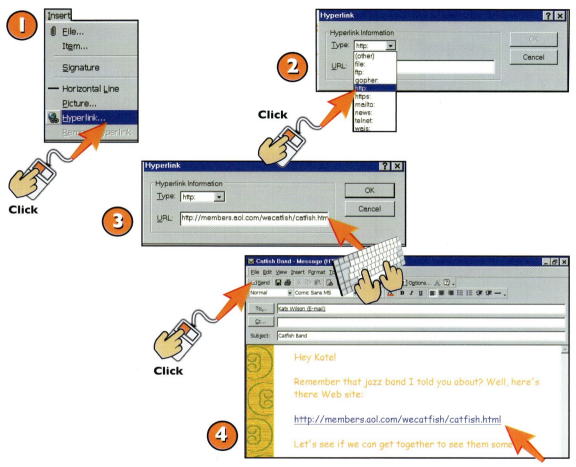

You can share a piece of the Internet with a colleague by inserting a link in a message to a page on the World Wide Web. When the recipient clicks the hyperlink, his or her *Web browser* starts and connects to the address you've entered. This is a nice way to share some information you may have found. You can also use this same technique to point a recipient to a page on your company's intranet (private "Internet").

(!) WARNING
You must create an HTML message or a message with Stationery to insert a hyperlink.

(✓) Other Links
You can use this same technique to insert other links, such as a link to an ftp (file download) site or a mailto link (a link that creates an email message to the person whose address you enter.)

① Open the **Insert** file and select **Hyperlink**.

② Select **http:** from the **Type** list.

③ Type the location of the Web page in the **URL** text box, like this: `http://members.aol.com/wecatfish/catfish.hmtl` and click **OK**.

④ The link appears as hypertext. Click **Send**.

Task 12: Creating an Office Document and Sending it in a Message

If you need to send someone a file, but you haven't actually created that file yet, you can create an Office *document* and send it to someone in a short series of steps. Outlook makes all of the application's menus and tools available, such as the Formula Bar in Excel or the Table menu in Word. You might use this task to create a small worksheet, chart, or a simple Word document to send to a colleague. You won't be able to type a message, so if that's a problem, create the file as usual and simply attach it. (See Part 2, Task 9.)

✓ Run for Office

Both you and the recipient must have other Office components installed, such as Word or Excel, to complete this task. If the recipient does not use Office, see Part 2, Task 1 for an alternative.

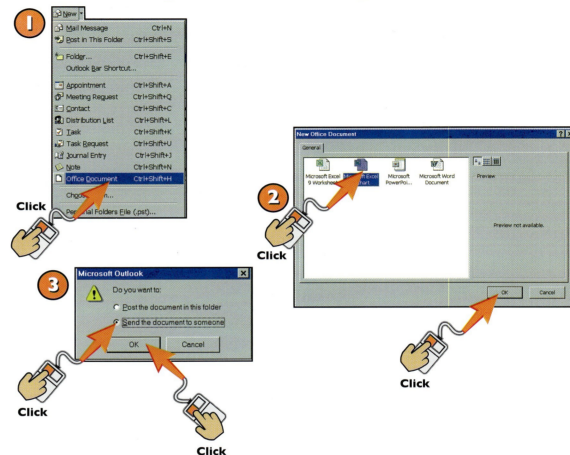

Start Here

Click

Click

Click

Click

① Click the arrow on the **New** button, and select **Office Document**.

② Select the template for the document you want to create, and click **OK**.

③ Click **Send the document to someone** and click **OK**.

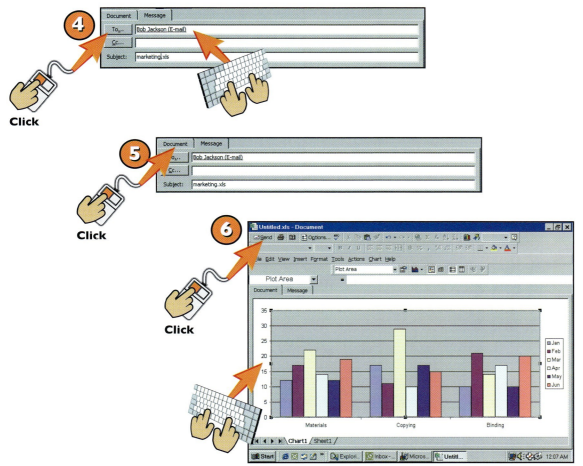

Click

Click

Click

4 Enter an address in the **To** box, and a name for the document in the **Subject** box.

5 Click the **Document** tab.

6 Create the document, and then click **Send**.

 Other Uses
You can use this same process to post a new document to a **Public or Net Folder** so it can be shared. Just select **Post the document in this folder** in step 3.

 End Task

Task 13: Creating an Office Document and Sending it in an Envelope

If your colleague does not use Office, he or she will not be able to view any office documents you simply send. So create the Office document and send it in an "envelope" instead. When you tell Outlook to send the document, its contents are converted to **MIME HTML (MHTML)** text and placed inside a message. The recipient will not have to have Office on his or her system to display the contents of the message because it is just enhanced text.

✅ **Need Your Office**
You must have other Office components installed, such as Word or Excel, to complete this task.

⚠️ **WARNING**
Because this task creates an HTML message, the recipient must have an email program that supports HTML.

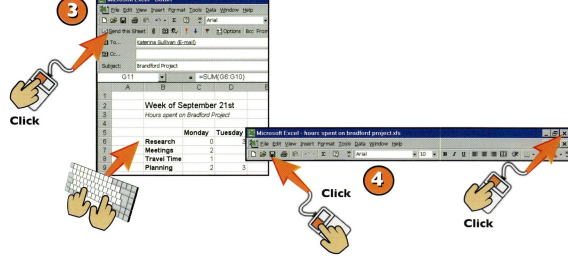

① Open the **Actions** menu, select **New Mail Message Using**, select **Microsoft Office**, and then select the type of document you want to create.

② Enter an address in the **To** box and a description in the **Subject** box.

③ Create the document and click **Send this Sheet**.

④ Click **Save** to save the document if you want, and then click **Close** to exit the program.

Task 14: Attaching an Outlook Item to a Message

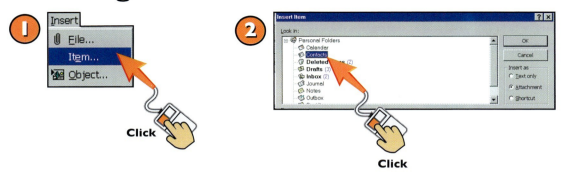

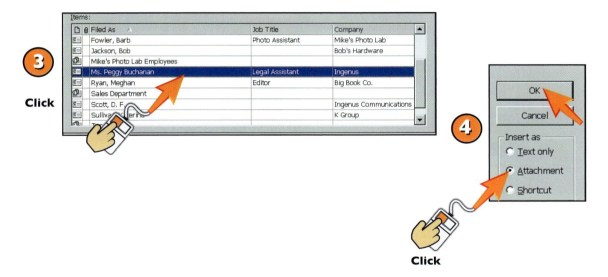

In addition to attaching files to your messages, you can attach Outlook items as well. For example, you can attach a contact or *task* item to a message to share with a colleague. However, the recipient must have Outlook to view any items you send him. If he doesn't have Outlook, you can send the contents of the item as text. If you're both connected to the same network, you can send a *shortcut* that points to the item instead—the recipient then double-clicks the shortcut icon and the item is displayed.

Click

Click

Click

Click

① Open the **Insert** menu and select **Item**.

② Click the folder that contains the item you want to insert.

③ Click the item you want to insert.

④ Select **Attachment**, **Text only**, or **Shortcut**, and then click **OK**.

✔ **Quick Way to Insert an Item**
You can also insert an item by simply dragging it into an open message or (to create a new message) by dragging it onto the Inbox folder.

Task 15: Adding an AutoSignature

A *Signature* is a text file that you can insert into your messages. It can contain your name, company, email address, and other pertinent information you want to include with your messages on a regular basis. By creating a signature file, you can simply insert this information instead of retyping it each time you want to create a new message.

✓ **Use it Again**

To use the signature in another email message, open the **Insert** menu, select **Signature**, and then select the signature you want to use.

! **WARNING**

If you use **Word** as your email editor, start an email message. Then open the **Tools** menu, select **Options**, click the **General** tab, and click **Email options** to create a signature.

Start Here

Click

Click

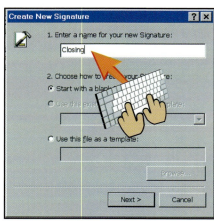

1 Open the **Insert** menu, select **Signature**, and then select **More**.

2 Click **Yes.**

3 Type a name for the signature file.

Next Step

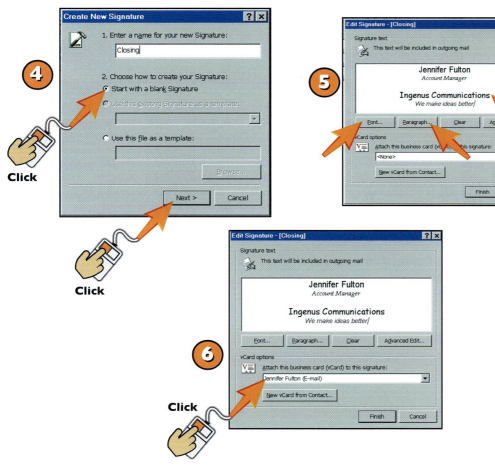

More Than One
You can create multiple signature files. Open the **Tools** menu, select **Options**, click the **Mail Format** tab, and click **Signature Picker**. Click **New** to create another signature file.

Always Add A Signature
To insert a signature in all email messages, open the **Tools** menu, select **Options**, click the **Mail Format** tab, and select the signature from the **Use this Signature by default** list.

4 Select **Start with a blank Signature**. Click **Next>**.

5 Type the text you want to use as your *AutoSignature*. Use the **Font** and **Paragraph** buttons to format the text.

6 Select a vCard to attach to the signature if you want. Click **Finish.**

Task 16: Checking Spelling

Everyone makes typographical and spelling errors at one time or another. But it would be a shame to let these errors ruin your message. Fortunately, Outlook's spell checking utility makes it easy to find and fix your spelling errors. Outlook even enables you to add your own words to its built-in dictionary.

Click

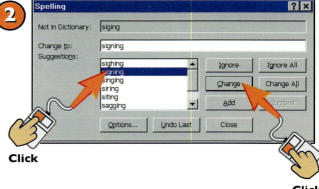

Click

Click

✔ **Watch Your Grammar**
If you're using Word as your email editor, its spelling checker can check your grammar too. As a result, its dialog box looks a bit different than this one, but the buttons function in the same manner as described here.

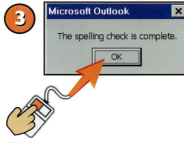

Click

✔ **Check Before You Send**
To have Outlook automatically check your messages before you send them, open the **Tools** menu, select **Options**, and then click the **Spelling** tab. Select **Always check spelling before sending** and click **OK**.

1 Open the **Tools** menu and select **Spelling** or press **F7**.

2 Select a suggestion and click **Change** or **Change All.** To ignore the word, click **Ignore** or **Ignore All.** Click **Add** to add the word to the dictionary.

3 Click **OK**.

Task 17: Adding Voting Buttons to a Message

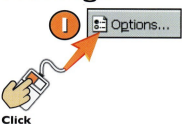

Click

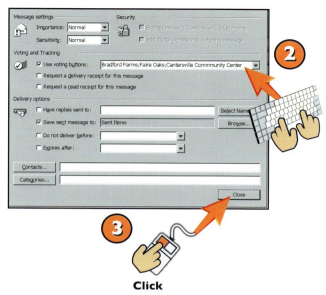

Click

You can attach *voting buttons* to a message, and your recipients can then vote on various propositions, such as a salary cut, a benefits change, and so on. The buttons look the same as those you'd find in a dialog box. When the user opens your message, he simply clicks the button of his choice, and a reply is sent back to you.

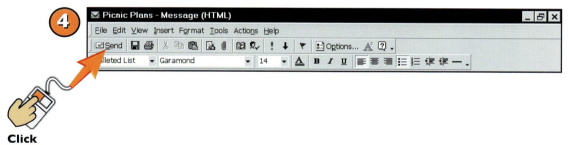

Click

1. Click the **Options** button.

2. Select the **Use voting buttons** option, and then select from the list or type the button names you want.

3. Click **Close**.

4. Click **Send** to send your email message.

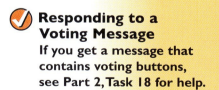

Responding to a Voting Message
If you get a message that contains voting buttons, see **Part 2, Task 18 for help.**

Counting the Votes
If you need help counting the responses to your vote, see **Part 2, Task 19.**

Task 18: Responding to a Voting Message

Since adding voting buttons to a message is so easy (see Part 2, Task 17), you may be asked for your opinion more often! As you'll see in this task, it's easy to cast your vote: just click the response you want to send. In addition, you can accompany your vote with a short message.

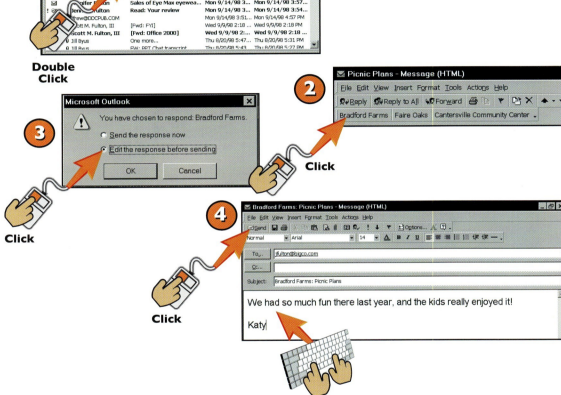

Double Click

Click

Click

Click

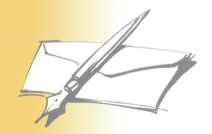

①　Double-click the message to open it.

②　Click the button that represents your choice.

③　Select whether or not to send a message with your vote, and click **OK**.

④　If you decided to send a message, address it and type your response. Then click **Send**.

Task 19: Checking Responses to a Voting Message

Click

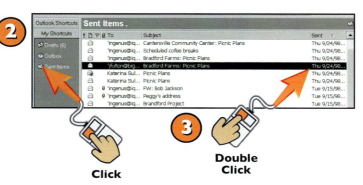

Click

Double Click

After you send out a request for a vote, all you have to do is sit back, relax, and tally up the ballots. When someone responds to your voting message, you'll receive an email message in your inbox. The message contains a notation that tells you how that person has voted; you may or may not see an additional message.

---

1 Click **My Shortcuts.**

2 Click the **Sent Items** folder.

3 Double-click the response to open it.

4 You'll see a message at the top of the window telling you how that person voted.

 Get Out and Vote!
If you want to send a voting message and you're not sure how, see **Part 2, Task 17.**

Task 20: Manually Checking for New Messages

If you receive your email through your company's network, Outlook periodically checks for new mail and notifies you when it arrives. However, if you use a remote mail server, you must periodically check for messages yourself by connecting to the server and downloading (receiving) new mail. In addition, even if you are connected by network to the mail server, you may want to check for new mail immediately, instead of waiting until the next timed interval. If you have any outgoing messages in the Outbox when you check for messages, they are automatically sent.

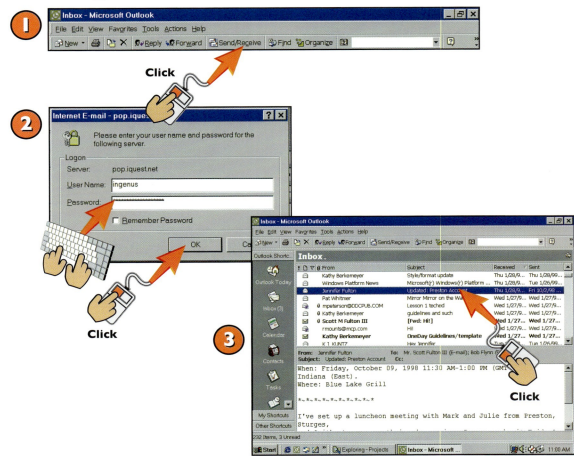

Click **Send and Receive**.

If prompted, type your password and click **OK**.

New messages appear in the Inbox, typically at the top of the window. Unread messages are highlighted in bold text. To view a message, in the previous pane at the bottom of the window, click it.

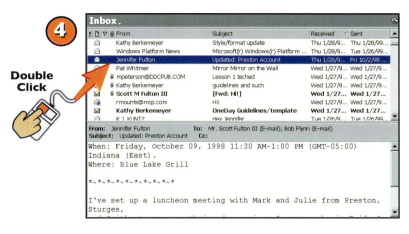

Double Click

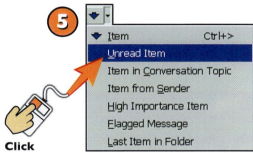

Click

✓ **Checking Automatically**
If you want to adjust the interval at which Outlook checks for mail, open the **Tools** menu, select **Options**, and click the **Internet Email** tab. At the bottom of the page are several options for setting the checking interval and allowing Outlook to dial up automatically to check mail.

✓ **Got New Mail!**
If your mail is delivered automatically, how do you know when new mail arrives? Well, first, you'll hear a beep. An envelope icon appears on the Windows taskbar. Double-click this icon to display the Inbox, if it is not already displayed.

4 To view a message in a full window, double-click it.

5 To view the next unread item, click the arrow on the **Next Item** button and select **Unread Item**.

If you're often out of the office on business, there's no reason why you can't still receive your email messages. With remote email, you can use your laptop to dial up your messaging service, obtain a listing of your messages, mark the ones you want to receive right now, and then download (receive) the messages you marked. Of course, Outlook must be installed on the laptop, and your messaging service must be setup (see Appendix A, "Installing Outlook 2000").

⚠ WARNING

Typically, when a message is received, it is removed from the mail server. So if you need to be able to retrieve this message again (on your office PC), use the **Mark to Retrieve a Copy** button in step to get a copy of the message instead (and leave the original on the server). To get rid of a message you don't want, use the **Delete** button to mark it.

Task 21: Checking for Messages Remotely

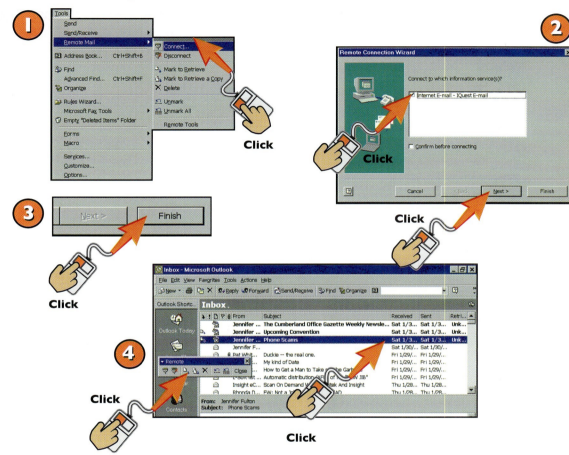

Open the **Tools** menu, select **Remote Mail**, and then select **Connect**.

Select the messaging service(s) you want to check. Click **Next>**.

Click **Finish.** The headers for new messages are downloaded to your PC.

Click the header for a message you wish to download, and then click the **Mark to Retrieve** button.

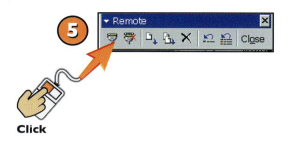

Click

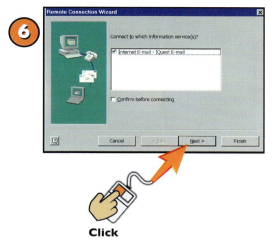

Click

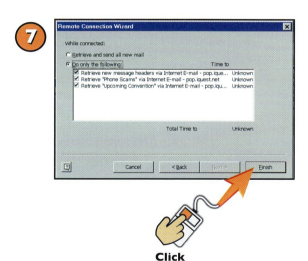

Click

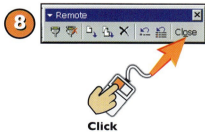

Click

Click

✅ **What Happened?**
Only the contents for the messages you select in step 4 will be downloaded. The headers (only) for the remaining messages will continue to appear in the Inbox until you exit Outlook.

✅ **But I Want All My Mail!**
If you want to send and receive all your mail without looking at your message headers, click the **Retrieve and send all new mail** option in step 3.

5 Click **Connect**.

6 The messaging service(s) you marked earlier should still be marked, so simply click **Next>**.

7 Click **Finish**. You're connected to the service(s) you selected, and the messages you marked are retrieved.

8 Click **Close**.

End
Task

Task 22: Reading Your Messages

When a new message comes in, you can view its contents. After reading a message, you can reply to it, forward it, file it, or print it. Also, after reading the message, you can delete it from your system.

Start Here

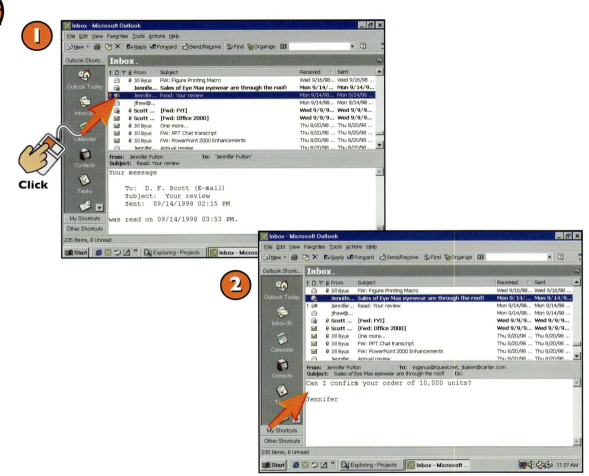

Click

① Click the message whose contents you want to view. (Unread messages appear in **bold** text.)

② The contents of the message appears in the Preview Page.

Task 23: Using AutoPreview

Start Here

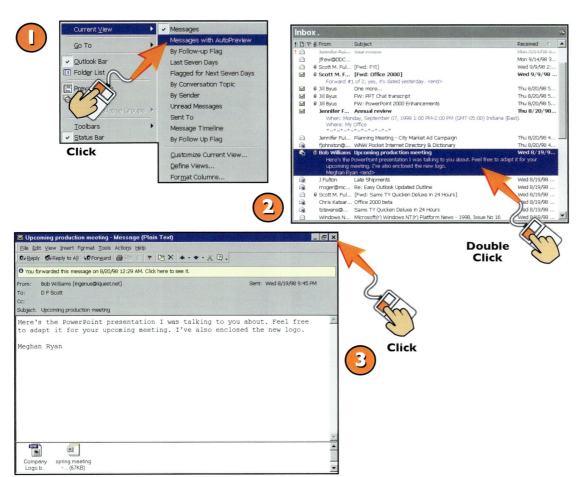

Click

②

③ **Click**

Double Click

Wish you could know what a message contains before you take the time to read it? If so, use *AutoPreview* to display an excerpt (a small paragraph) from each unread message, and then read only the messages you absolutely need to right now.

① Open the **View** menu, select **Current View**, and then select **Messages with AutoPreview**.

② Double-click an unread message to view its full contents.

③ After viewing the message, click its **Close** button.

✓ **Too Much?**
When you use AutoPreview, the Preview Page is automatically turned off to create more room in the message listing.

✓ **Just Another View**
AutoPreview is just another view, a way in which you can display your messages. To change to a different view, see Part 1, Task 6 for help.

End Task

Task 24: Reading a Message in a Public Folder

A *public folder's* contents shared by everyone in your company through the network. You might find public notices (posted as messages) in a public folder or other documents such as company letters and reports, sales and production worksheets, and company presentations. In this way, a public folder acts as an electronic bulletin board, disseminating important company information quickly. Depending on your level of access, you can view the folder's contents and possibly post your own data to the folder as well.

✅ **Go Public!**
If you would like to share your Inbox with others, see Part 2, Task 37. To share your *Calendar*, see Part 3, Task 14.

✅ **What's Your Response?**
After viewing a public message, respond as to a personal message. See Part 2, Task 26 for help.

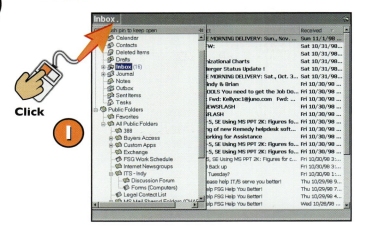

Click

Click

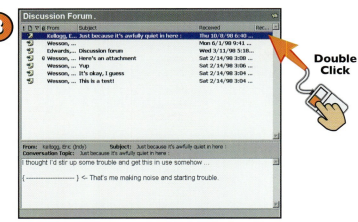

Double Click

1 Open the **Folder List**.

2 Click the public folder whose contents you wish to view.

3 Double-click a message to view its contents.

Task 25: Posting a Response to a Conversation

Start Here

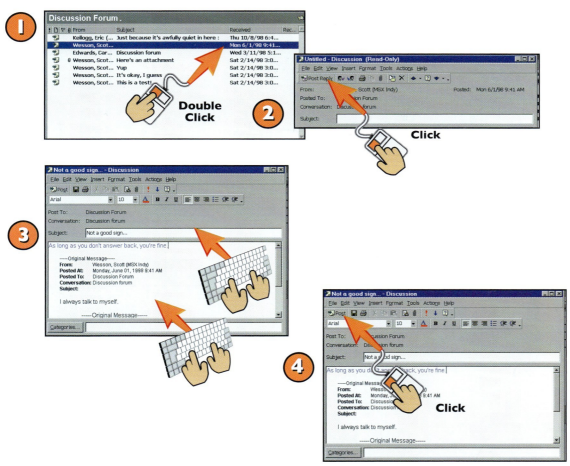

Double Click

Click

What's a Conversation?

When someone views a message in a public folder and replies to it, he creates a *conversation* or *thread*, which links similar messages to each other. Later on, another person can follow the thread of the conversation by reading the related messages in order. If you want to add your "two cents" to a conversation, all you need to do is reply to a message.

✓ **Following a Thread**
To view messages within the same conversation, open the **View** menu, select **Current View**, and then select **By Conversation Topic**. To reveal the messages within a topic, click its plus sign.

❗ **WARNING**
You may not have *permission* to post messages within certain public folders.

1 Double-click the message to which you wish to respond.

2 Click **Post Reply**.

3 Type a **Subject** and your response.

4 Click **Post**.

End Task

Task 26: Starting a New Conversation in a Public Folder

Starting a New Thread

Messages that follow the same topic form a *thread* or *conversation*. Specifically, a thread is created when someone posts a message with a unique subject line, and someone else posts a reply to that message. If you have a unique topic you wish to discuss, rather than replying to an existing message (and adding to that thread), begin your own conversation.

⚠️ **WARNING**

Before you begin a new conversation (thread), you should check other messages to make sure your topic is unique. To view messages by conversation, open the **View** menu, select **Current View**, and then select **By Conversation Topic**.

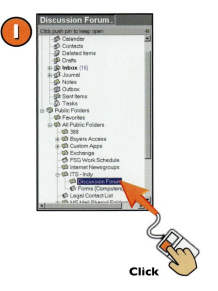

Click

Click

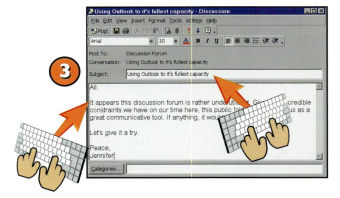

① Click the folder to which you wish to post your message.

② Click **New Post**.

③ Type a **Subject** for your message. (Make sure that it's unique.)

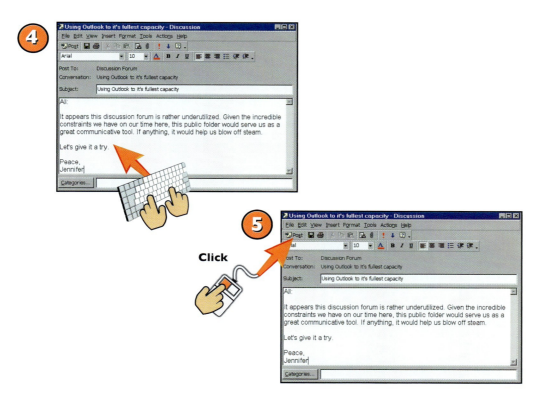

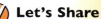

Click

Let's Share
If you want to share a file with your colleagues, you can post it to a public folder. Just drag the file into an open folder. To create a new **Office** document, follow the steps in **Part 2, Task 12**, but select **Post the document in this folder.**

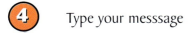

Type your messsage

Click **Post**.

Task 27: Flagging Messages You've Read

After reading your messages, you can *flag* the ones that are important to you. For example, if a particular message requires a follow-up, or if it contains important information you don't want to forget, place a flag on it.

Start Here

Click

✓ **Select a Flag**
In addition to marking a message as important or sensitive (as you learned to do in Part 2, Task 4), you can also add flags (such as **Review** or **Call**) to messages you're sending. Just follow these same steps; the flag appears at the top of the message window.

Click

Click

① Select the message you wish to flag.

② Open the **Actions** menu and select **Flag for Follow Up**.

③ Select a flag from the **Flag to** list.

Next Step

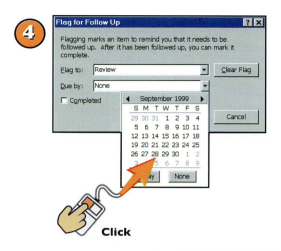

Click

Click

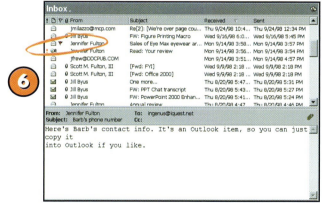

In My Own Words, Please!
If you don't see a flag you like, type your own in the text box.

Removing a Flag
Once you've performed the follow-up action, you can remove the flag from the message. See Part 2, Task 28 for help.

④ If you want, select a due date for the flag from the **Due by** list. You can edit the time as needed.

⑤ Click **OK**.

⑥ A flag appears in front of the message in the Inbox window. The flag also appears above the text in the message window.

End Task

Task 28: Removing a Flag

After reviewing a message that's marked with a flag, you may want to remove the flag or mark it as "completed" so you don't attempt to perform the same follow-up again. For example, if a message was marked for later review and you've performed that review, mark that message as completed or remove its flag. If you mark a message as completed, its flag appears in green rather than red.

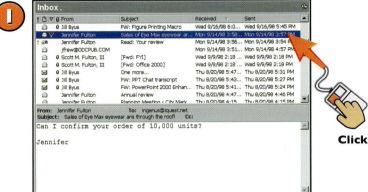

Click

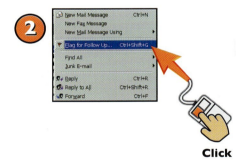

Click

Click

✅ **All in Your Point of View**
To quickly review messages that are flagged, open the **View** menu, select **Current View**, and then select **By Follow-up Flag**.

⚠️ **WARNING**
To remove a flag, follow these same steps, but click **Clear Flag** in step 3.

1 Select the message whose flag you wish to remove.

2 Open the **Actions** menu and select **Flag for Follow Up**.

3 Click **Completed**, and click OK. To remove the flag, click **Clear Flag** instead.

Task 29: Opening an Attached File

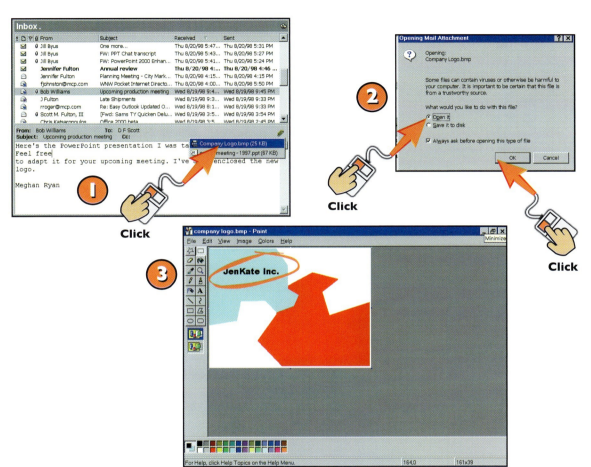

Click

Click

Click

If someone has attached a file to one of your messages, you can easily view its contents, even prior to saving the file to your hard disk. (Messages with attached files are marked with a paper clip icon.) To view the file, however, you must have a program that is compatible with it. For example, if someone attaches an Excel worksheet to a message, you can view it provided you have Excel or a program that's compatible with it, such as Lotus 1-2-3.

① Click the **paper clip** icon and select the file you wish to open.

② If a dialog box appears, select **Open it** and click **OK**.

③ The file opens within its associated program.

 Saving the Attached File

You may want to save the file to your hard disk prior to viewing it, especially if you plan on making any changes. See Part 2, Task 30 for help.

Task 30: Saving an Attached File

In Part 2, Task 29, you learned how to open an attached file so you can view it. However, you might want to save the attached file to your hard drive before you open it. Although you can open an attached file (and even make changes to it) without saving the file to your hard drive first, if you don't save the file to your hard drive at some point, your changes will be lost. By the way, messages that contain attached files appear with a small paper clip icon.

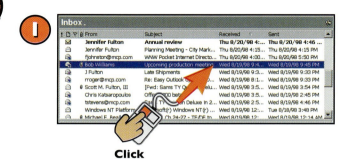

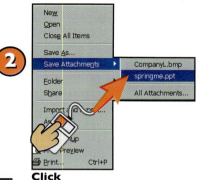

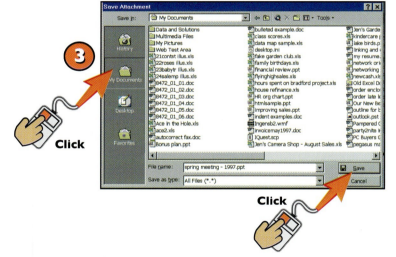

✔️ **Saving Several Attachments**
To save several attachments to the same folder, open the **File** menu, select **Save Attachments**, and then select **All Attachments**.

✔️ **What's in a Name?**
You can rename the file as you're saving it by typing a new name for the file in the **File name** text box.

1 Select the message that contains the file you wish to save.

2 Open the **File** menu, select **Save Attachments**, and then select the file you wish to save.

3 Select the folder in which you want to save the file, and then click **Save**.

Task 31: Replying to a Message

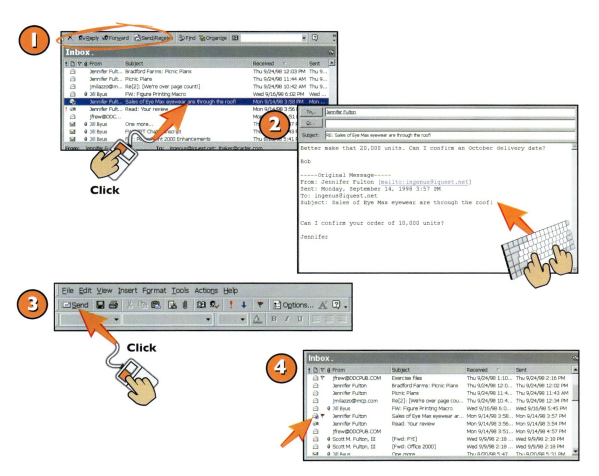

Click

Click

When you reply to a message, the original message is copied to your reply. This helps the recipient remember the words to which you are referring. You can send your reply to just the originator or to the originator and all the recipients of the original message.

⚠️ **WARNING**
Although it's copied to your reply, you can delete the text of the original message if you like. Just drag over the text to select it, and then press **Delete**.

✔️ **Saving a Contact**
To add the *sender* of a message to **Contacts**, open the message, right-click in the **To** field on the name you wish to save, and then select **Add to Contacts**.

✔️ **Time to Vote?**
If you need to reply to a message that includes voting buttons, see Part 2, Task 18.

1. Select the message to which you want to reply, and click **Reply**.

2. Type your reply above the original message.

3. Click **Send**.

4. The message appears with an open envelope icon with a small red arrow.

Page **61**

You might forward a message if it was sent to the wrong person, if the project to which it refers has been reassigned to someone else, or if you know of someone who should be made aware of its information. Unlike a reply, which is automatically addressed to the originator of the message, you can forward a message to anyone you wish.

✓ **Multiple Messages**
You can forward multiple messages to the same people at one time, but they will be sent as attachments, not as individual messages. To select multiple messages, press and hold the **Ctrl** key as you click each one.

✓ **Multiple People**
You can forward your message to more than one person. If you're typing the addresses manually, be sure to separate them with a semi-colon (;).

Task 32: Forwarding a Message

Click   **Click**

Click

1 Select the message you want to forward, and click **Forward.**

2 In the **To** text box, type the address of the person to whom you wish to forward the message.

3 Type a message in the text area. Click **Send**.

4 The message you've forwarded appears with an open envelope icon with a small blue arrow.

Task 33: Sending a Fax

Start Here

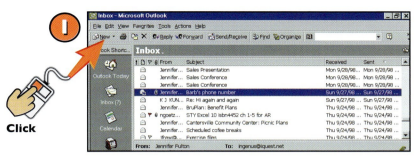

Click

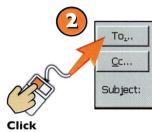

Click

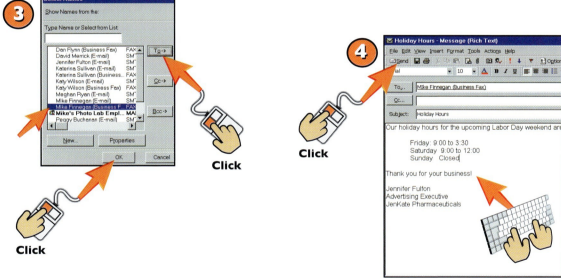

Click

Click

Click

If your PC has a fax modem, you can send a *fax* directly from your computer. You can also receive faxes directly (see Part 2, Task 34). The most obvious reason for using Outlook to coordinate your faxes is the convenience: no more trips to the fax machine, no more waiting in line, and no more lost faxes. Sending a fax is similar to sending an email message.

(!) WARNING
To use this feature, you must have the Microsoft Fax service installed. See Appendix A for help.

✓ Better Fax?
You can use Word to create your fax document, and have Outlook send it. See Part 2, Task 12.

✓ Need a Fax Number
The address you select in step 3 must be marked with a notation (Business Fax). To add the fax number for a contact, see Part 4, Task 2 for help.

1 Click the **New Mail Message** button.

2 Click the **To** button.

3 Select the person to whom you want to send a fax, click **To**, and then click **OK**.

4 Type a **Subject** and your message. Click **Send**.

End Task

Task 34: Receiving a Fax

You can receive faxes with Outlook, view them, and even print them out. Outlook can automatically answer the phone and receive faxes, or you can control the process manually.

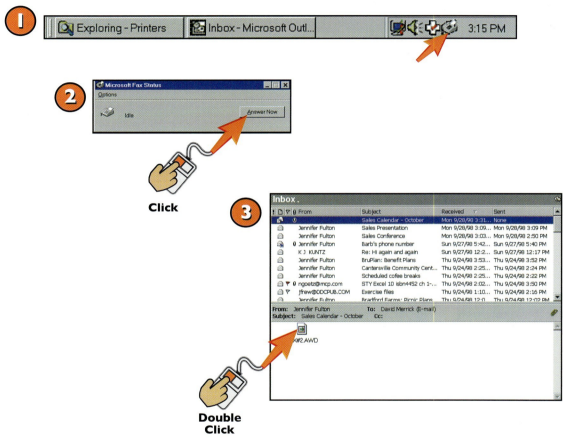

Click

Double
Click

WARNING

To use this feature, you must have the Microsoft Fax service installed. See Appendix A for help.

WARNING

By default, Microsoft Fax is not set up to answer incoming calls. To set Microsoft Fax up to do so, right-click the **Fax** icon that appears on the Windows taskbar. Select **Modem Properties**, and under **Answer mode**, select **Answer after X rings.**

1 To receive faxes, Outlook must be running. The fax icon on the taskbar lets you know that everything is ready.

2 If Microsoft Fax is not set up to answer automatically, when a fax machine dials your modem, click **Answer Now**.

3 To view a fax, double-click the fax icon.

Next
Step

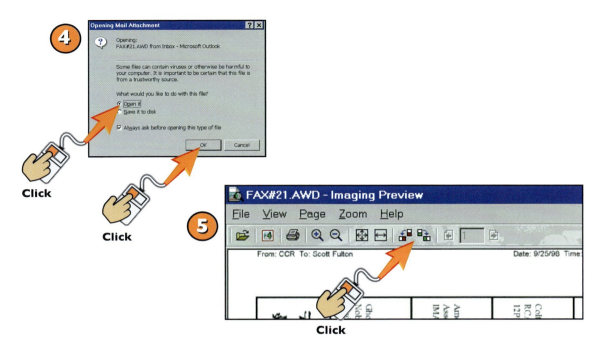

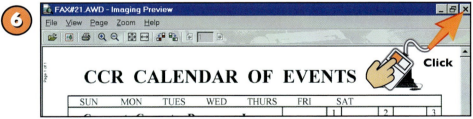

4 Click **Open it**, and then click **OK**.

5 If needed, click the **Rotate Left** or **Rotate Right** buttons to display the message so you can read it.

6 When you're done viewing the fax, click the **Close** button.

✓ **Viewing Fax Messages**
If you received a fax that was sent as a message (instead of something sent by a real fax machine), when you double-click it, it will open like an ordinary message and you can read it as usual.

Task 35: Allowing Someone Else to Answer Your Mail

Delegating Your Mail

If you have an office assistant that handles your incoming paper mail, you can have your assistant handle your Outlook mail as well. You can grant various levels of access, but this task assumes you want your assistant to be able to read, create, and delete mail as needed.

Start Here

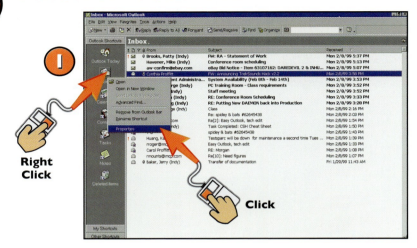

Right Click

Click

Click

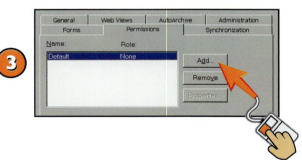

Click

⚠️ **WARNING**

Your company must use Microsoft Exchange Server as its email server for you to perform this task.

✓ **More Access**

You can grant access to your Calendar, Contacts, and *Tasks* lists as well; see upcoming tasks: Part 3, Task 14 (Calendar), Part 4, Task 19 (Contacts), and Part 5, Task 9 (Tasks) for help.

1 Right-click the **Inbox** folder and select **Properties**.

2 Click the **Permissions** tab.

3 Click **Add**.

Next Step

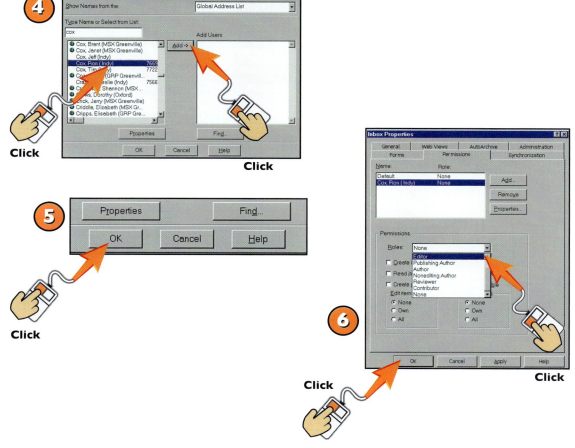

Click

Click

Click

Click

Click

④ Select the person you want to grant access to and click **Add**.

⑤ Click **OK**.

⑥ Select **Editor** from the **Roles** list. Click **OK**.

✓ **View Only, Please**
If you want to grant someone permission to review your mail but not to create or delete mail, see Part 2, Task 36 for help.

Task 36: Allowing Others to View Your Mail

If you would like to have the convenience of knowing if you've received any important mail while you're out of the office, but you don't need anyone to reply to your email on your behalf, you can grant them permission to view your mail only.

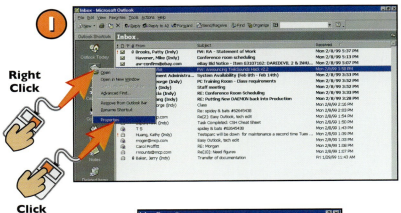

Right Click

Click

Click

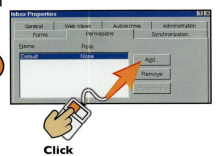

Click

Start Here

⚠ **WARNING**

Your company must use **Microsoft Exchange Server** as its email server for you to perform this task.

✓ **View Only, Please**

If you want to grant someone permission to review your mail and create replies, but not to delete or edit your mail, select **Nonediting Author** from the **Roles** list.

1 Right-click the **Inbox** folder and select **Properties**.

2 Click the **Permissions** tab.

3 Click **Add**.

Next Step

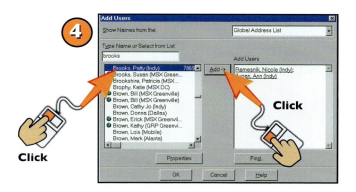

Click

Click

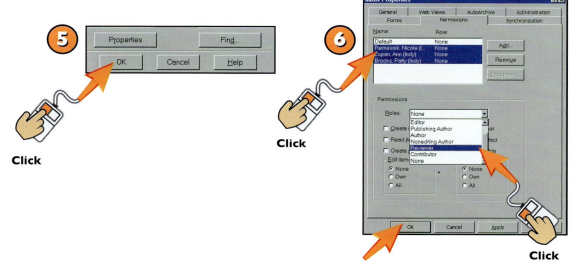

Click

Click

Click

4 Select the person you want to grant access to and click **Add**.

5 Click **OK**.

6 Select the person in the **Name** list, select **Reviewer** from the **Roles** list, and click **OK**.

Task 37: Opening Someone Else's Mail

Viewing Someone's Mail

If you've been granted access to someone else's mail, you can open it just as you might your own mail. With additional permission, you can even reply to messages and delete outdated or irrelevant messages as well.

⊘ **WARNING**
Your company must use Microsoft Exchange Server as its email server for you to perform this task. In addition, you must be given access to another person's Inbox.

✔ **Automatic Open**
To have Outlook automatically open someone else's Inbox every time you start Outlook, select **Tools Services**. Select **Microsoft Exchange Server**, and click **Properties**. Click the **Advanced** tab, and click **Add**. Type the name of the mailbox you want to open, and then click **OK**. Click **OK** again.

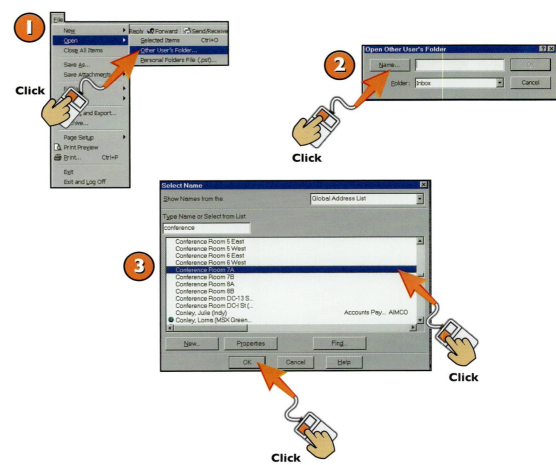

Start Here

Click

Click

Click

Click

Open the **File** menu, select **Open**, and then select **Other User's Folder**.

Click **Name**.

Select the name of the person who's Inbox you wish to view and click **OK**.

Next Step

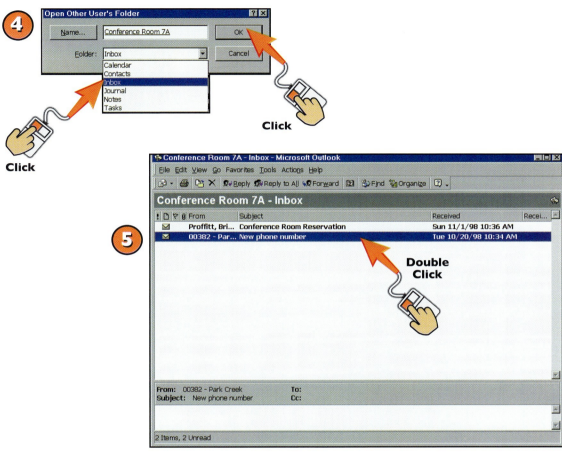

Click

Click

Double Click

④ In the **Folder** list, click **Inbox** and click **OK**.

⑤ To view a particular message, double-click it.

After you start receiving messages, you'll want to organize them. This enables you to quickly act on important messages, and to keep track of others that are not as important but still relevant. One way to organize your messages is with color. Outlook allows you to color messages coming from a particular person (such as your boss) or going to a particular person (such as an associate for whom you are managing mail). In addition, you can highlight with color messages that are addressed solely to you (as opposed to a *group* message).

Task 38: Organizing the Inbox with Colors

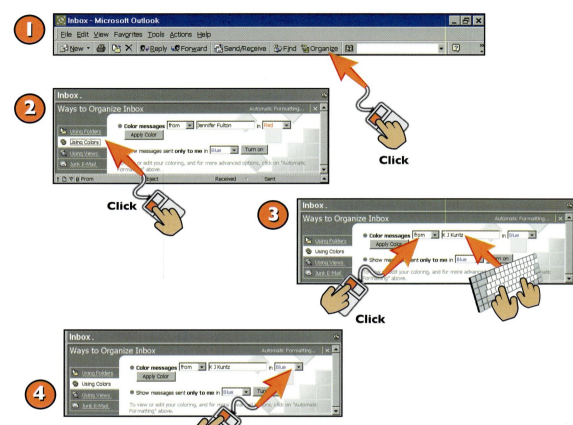

✅ **Tired of Color?**
If you want to get rid of a color format you've added, click Automatic Formatting, select the condition you want to remove, and click Delete.

1 Click **Organize**.

2 Click **Using Colors**.

3 To highlight messages from/to a particular person, select **From** or **To**, and type that person's name in the text box.

4 Select a color from the list.

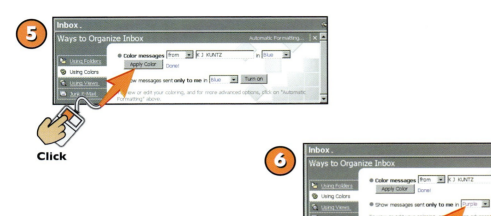

Click

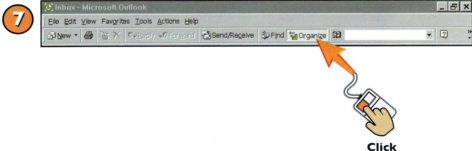

Click   Click

Click

5 Click **Apply Color**.

6 To highlight messages sent only to you, select a color from the list and click **Turn on**.

7 Click **Organize** to return to the Inbox.

✔ **Rinse and Repeat**
You can repeat steps 3, 4, and 5 to add **additional** names you wish to highlight.

✔ **More Color!**
Using the **Automatic Formatting** feature on the **Using Colors** tab, you can color unread, expired, overdue, and unsent messages as well. In addition, you can add your own definitions for messages you want to highlight.

End Task

Task 39: Stopping Junk Mail

It's bad enough that you get unsolicited advertisements mixed in with your regular mail, but to get *junk mail* is almost too much. Put a stop to the time-wasting, nerve-wracking *junk mail* mania by allowing Outlook to *filter* it out. Outlook can color the headers of incoming junk and adult content mail (making them easier for you to identify), or simply move them to a different folder (such as the **Deleted Items** folder) automatically.

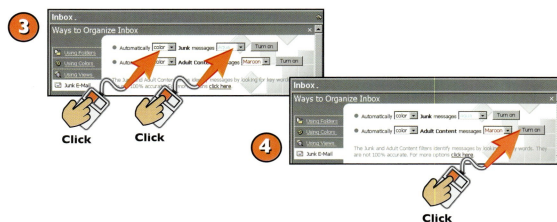

✅ **Help Outlook Help You**

You can help Outlook identify junk/adult content email by adding the name of a sender of such mail to a master list. If you accidentally receive junk/adult content mail after turning on this feature, right-click the message and select **Junk E-Mail** from the shortcut menu.

1 Click **Organize**.

2 Click **Junk E-Mail**.

3 To filter junk email, select **Color** or **Move** from the drop-down list.

4 Select a color or a folder from the second list. Click **Turn on**.

Next Step

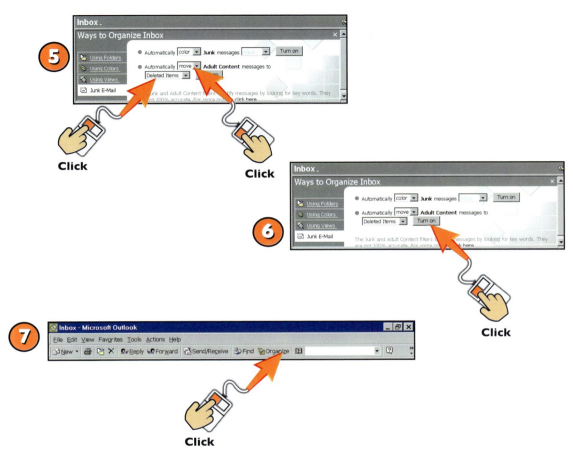

Click

Click

Click

Click

5 To filter adult content email, select **Color** or **Move** from the drop-down list.

6 Select a color or a folder from the second list. Click **Turn on**.

7 Click **Organize** to return to the Inbox.

✅ **But I Like Junk Mail!**
If you change your mind and decide you'd rather receive the junk email, return to the **Junk E-Mail** tab, and click **Turn off**.

✅ **More Rules**
With the **Tools/Rules Wizard** command, you can set up additional conditions to handle mail, such as flagging or moving particular messages.

✅ **Other Ways to Help**
Update Outlook's master list of junk/adult content mailers by downloading an update from the **Microsoft Web site**. Just click the **Click here** link on the **Junk E-Mail** tab, and then click **Outlook Web Site**.

Task 40: Printing a Message

You might want to print a message to take it with you to a *meeting* or an out-of-town conference. You might also want to print out a copy of a message for your files.

Start Here

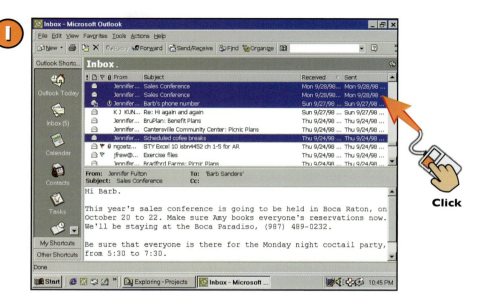

Click

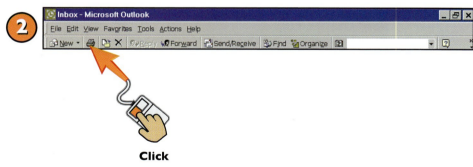

Click

1 Press and hold **Ctrl** as you click each message you want to print.

2 Click **Print**.

Next Step

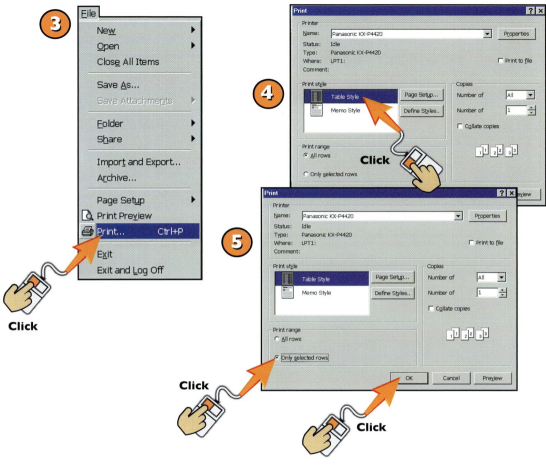

3 To print a listing of the message headers instead, open the **File** menu and select **Print**.

4 Select **Table Style**.

5 Select either **All rows** or **Only Selected Items** and click **OK**.

Tracking Appointments, Meetings, and Other Events with Calendar

You can keep track of all the important events in your life (meetings, appointments, anniversaries, birthdays, holidays, and so on) with the **Calendar**. In Outlook, an **appointment** does not involve inviting people within your organization or arranging for **resources** such as a meeting room, slide projector, and so on. A **meeting**, on the other hand, involves sending and receiving **meeting request**s, and scheduling meeting resources such as a room, A/V equipment, and so on. An **event** is an activity that lasts a day or more, such as a vacation, a convention, a trade show, a birthday, anniversary, special holiday, and so on.

When you schedule an appointment or meeting, you block out the amount of time you need, which prevents conflicts with other events. In addition, Outlook can remind you about the appointment or meeting before it occurs, so you can arrive on time.

Outlook also lets you schedule **recurring** events such as weekly or monthly meetings, workouts, doctor's appointments, salon visits, and so on. In addition, you can easily move appointments, meetings, and events when needed.

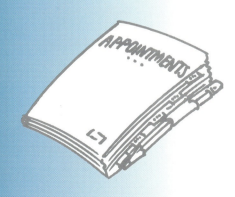

Tasks

Task 3: Scheduling an Appointment

An appointment is personal; it does not involve company personnel or resources, as a meeting might. You can schedule an appointment for any type of activity, such as a doctor's appointment, a lunch date, your workout, or a client meeting. By the way, an appointment that lasts all day is called an event. See Part 3, Task 6 for help in setting one up.

Start Here

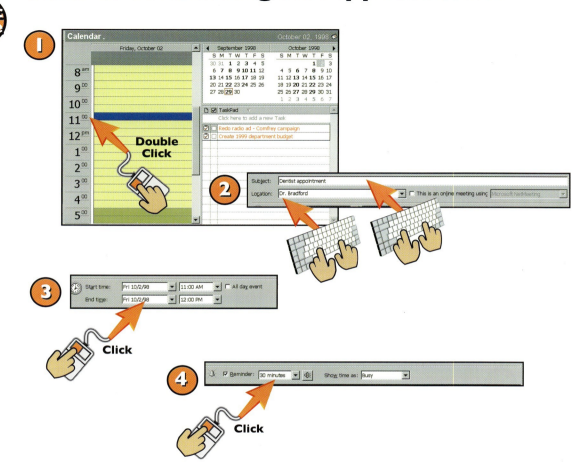

Double Click

Click

Click

✅ **Repeating Yourself?**
If you want to make this same appointment reoccur, see Part 3, Task 8.

✅ **Create an Appointment from a Message**
Drag an email *message* to the Calendar icon on the *Outlook bar* to create an appointment with its *sender*.

1 Double-click the time at which you want the appointment to occur.

2 Type a description for the appointment in the **Subject** text box. Enter a location in the **Location** text box.

3 Enter an end date and time.

4 Select the number of minutes prior to the appointment when you want the **reminder** to go off.

Next Step

Tasks

Task 1: Selecting the Day You Want to View

Initially, Calendar displays the appointments, meetings, and events you have set up for today. To view appointments for another day, you'll need to change from one day to another by using the *Date Navigator*. The date currently being displayed appears in a gray square. Today's date is marked by a red outline. If a date appears in bold within the Date Navigator, you have an appointment, meeting, or event scheduled for that day.

✔ **Viewing More Than One Day at a Time**
If you want to display more than a single day's worth of appointments, see Part 3, Task 2.

✔ **Quick Month Change**
You can skip to the month you want to display by clicking the name of one of the two months being displayed and then choosing the month you want.

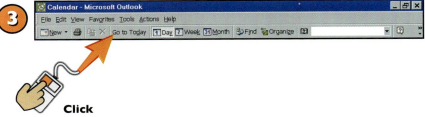

1 Click a date in the Date Navigator to display appointments for that date.

2 To display a month that's not visible, click the **left** or **right arrows** on the Date Navigator.

3 To view today's appointments, click **Go to Today**.

Task 2: Viewing a Week or a Month at a Time

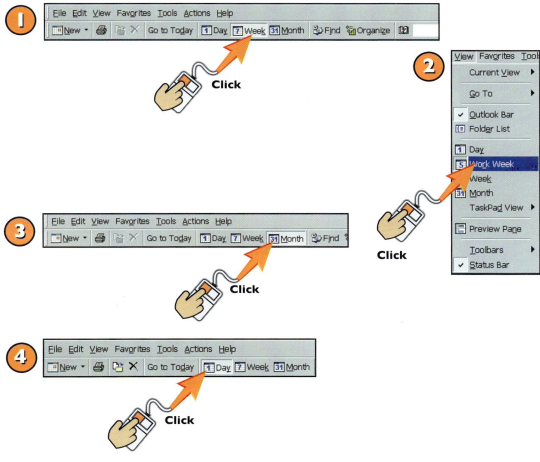

Click

Click

Click

Typically, Calendar displays only a single day's worth of appointments and meetings. However, if you want to review an entire week or the current month, you can do that easily. Viewing multiple days at one time makes it easy for you to adjust your time schedule.

1 To view a week's worth of appointments, click **Week**.

2 To view appointments for Monday to Friday only, open the view menu and select **Work Week**.

3 To view a month's worth of appointments, click **Month**.

4 To return to a single date display, click **Day**.

✓ **Viewing More Than One Day at a Time**
You can view particular days by pressing **Ctrl** and clicking the days you want to view in the **Date Navigator**.

✓ **What Week is This Anyway?**
If you like to know what week of the year it is, you can display week numbers in the Date Navigator by opening the **Tools** menu, selecting **Options**, clicking **Calendar Options**, and then selecting **Show week numbers in the Date Navigator**.

Task 3: Scheduling an Appointment

An appointment is personal; it does not involve company personnel or resources, as a meeting might. You can schedule an appointment for any type of activity, such as a doctor's appointment, a lunch date, your workout, or a client meeting. By the way, an appointment that lasts all day is called an event. See Part 3, Task 6 for help in setting one up.

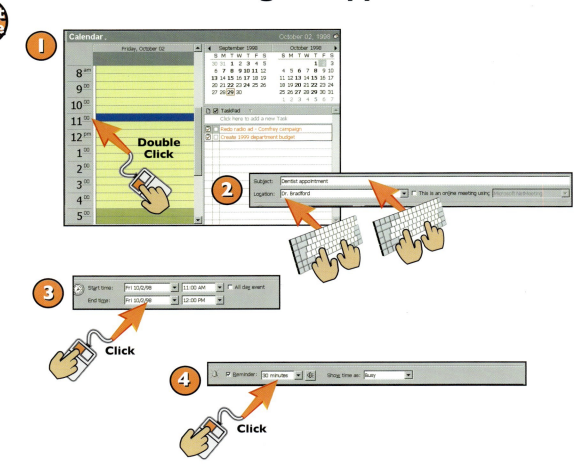

Start Here

Double Click

Click

Click

Repeating Yourself?
If you want to make this same appointment reoccur, see Part 3, Task 8.

Create an Appointment from a Message
Drag an email *message* to the Calendar icon on the *Outlook bar* to create an appointment with its *sender*.

1 Double-click the time at which you want the appointment to occur.

2 Type a description for the appointment in the *Subject* text box. Enter a location in the **Location** text box.

3 Enter an end date and time.

4 Select the number of minutes prior to the appointment when you want the *reminder* to go off.

Next Step

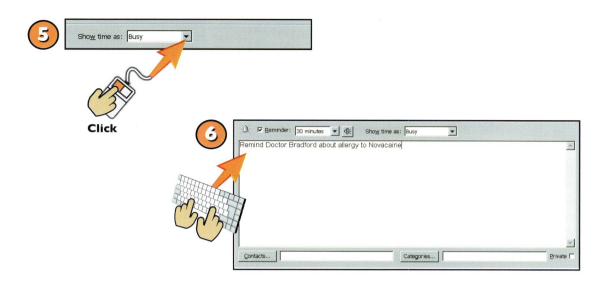

Click

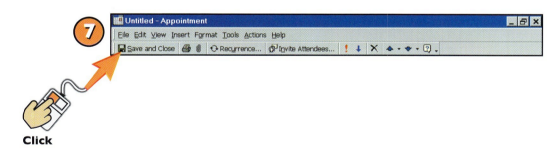

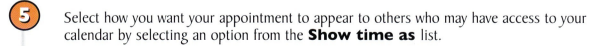

Click

5 Select how you want your appointment to appear to others who may have access to your calendar by selecting an option from the **Show time as** list.

6 Add any notes (such as directions, things to bring, and so on) in the large text box.

7 Click **Save and Close**.

✓ **What a Way to Organize!**
You can organize your appointments by *category* if you like. See Part 7, Task 7 for help.

✓ **Who's This Appointment With?**
You can *link* an appointment with a contact if you like. See Part 3, Task 4 for help.

Task 4: Associating a Contact Name with an Appointment

If your appointment is with someone in the *Contacts* list, you can associate the appointment with that contact name. Doing so might help you keep track of the number of hours spent with a client, for example, or enable you to quickly look up contact information while viewing the appointment in the Calendar. In addition, when needed, you can repeat these steps to associate as many contacts with an appointment as you like.

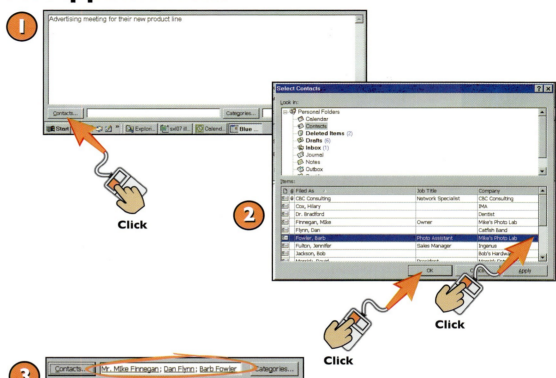

Start Here

Click

Click

Click

✓ **Quick Association**
To create a new appointment and associate it with a contact at the same time, drag the contact's name onto the **Calendar icon** in the Outlook bar.

1 Click the **Contacts** button.

2 Select the contact you wish to associate with this appointment, and click **OK**.

3 The name(s) you selected appear in the **Contacts** box.

Next Step

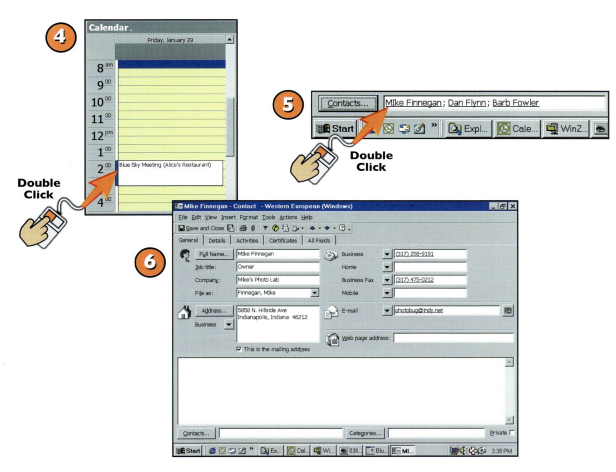

4 To look up contact information later, double-click the Appointment.

5 Double-click the contact name at the bottom of the window.

6 The contact information appears.

✓ **Multiple Contacts**
If you need to Associate multiple contacts with an appointment, select them one at a time in the Select Contacts dialog box, and click *Apply*. Click *OK* when you're through.

Task 5: Scheduling a Meeting

A meeting is an appointment that involves other company personnel. When you schedule a meeting, email requests are sent out over your company's *network*, inviting the people you selected to attend. When they respond to your request, their individual responses appear as email messages in your *Inbox*. However, you can access a summary of those responses through the **Meeting Planner** in the **Calendar**.

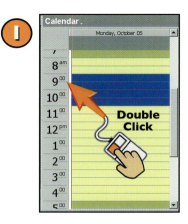

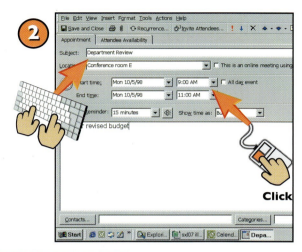

! WARNING
If you change your mind about the meeting prior to sending the invitations, click the **Cancel Invitation** button in the **Appointment** window. If you need to cancel a meeting later, see Part 3, Task 11 for help.

1 Double-click the meeting's start time.

2 Enter the **Subject**, **Location**, **End time**, **Reminder**, and other options just as you would for an appointment.

3 Click **Attendee Availability**.

4 Click **Invite Others**.

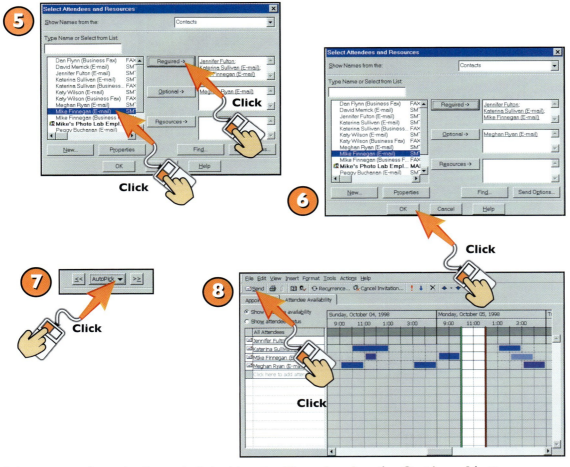

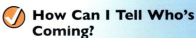

✅ **How Can I Tell Who's Coming?**

After attendees have responded to your meeting request, double-click the meeting and click the **Attendee Availability** tab. Click **Show attendee status**, and you'll see a listing of each individual's response.

✅ **What Do the Colors Mean?**

In the **Meeting Planner**, light blue indicates that the person is tentatively free, dark blue indicates that he or she is busy, and purple indicates that he or she is out of the office.

✅ **Schedule Resources Too**

If your network administrator has added the names of common resources (such as meeting rooms, projectors, and so on) to your company's address list, you can schedule them as well. Just select the item and click **Resources**.

5 Select a name from the list and click either the **Required** or the **Optional** button.

6 Repeat step 5 to invite additional people, and then click **OK**.

7 If needed, click **AutoPick** to have Outlook find a time when everyone is free.

8 Click **Send**. Invitations in the form of email messages are sent to each person listed.

Task 6: Scheduling an Event

An *event* is an activity that often takes place over an entire day or several days. Typical events include birthdays, anniversaries, and holidays. They also include seminars, all-day training sessions, conferences, retreats, and vacations. Events appear at the top of the day on which they occur. Individual time slots are not blocked out; the reasoning here is that often an event (such as a birthday) does not prevent you from attending other meetings or appointments.

⚠ **WARNING**
Normally, the time allotted to an event is shown as **Free** in your Calendar. You might want to change it to **Out of office** by selecting that option from the **Show time as** list.

✓ **Adding Holidays**
Standard holidays such as Christmas and New Year's are easy to add to Outlook. See Part 3, Task 13.

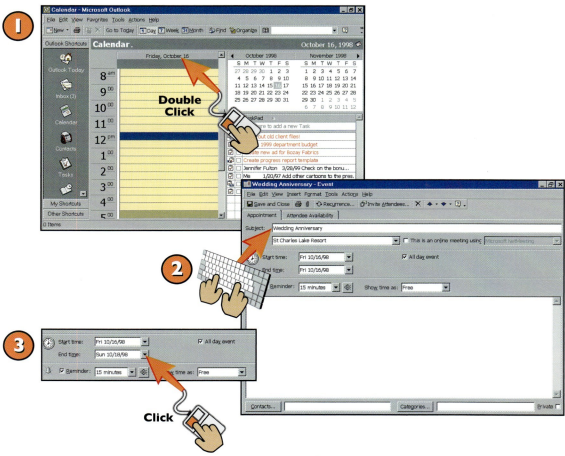

Double Click

Click

① Switch to the day on which the event will occur, and double-click on the date header.

② Type a name or description for the event in the **Subject** box. Enter a **Location** if applicable.

③ If the event occurs over several days, select an **End date** for the event. Also, if you like, you can add a note in the large text box.

Next Step

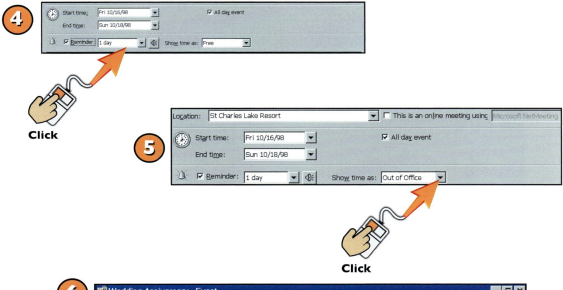

Click

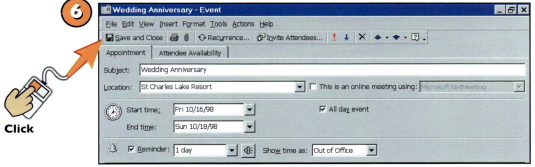

Click

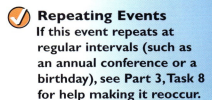

4 Set a **Reminder** if you want.

5 If you will not be attending appointments or meetings that day, select **Busy** or **Out of Office** from the **Show time as** list.

6 Click **Save and Close**.

✓ **Repeating Events**
If this event repeats at regular intervals (such as an annual conference or a birthday), see **Part 3, Task 8** for help making it reoccur.

End Task

The *Tasks* list (which you'll learn about in Part 5) helps you keep track of all the various things you need to do. But that still leaves you with the problem of finding the time in which to do everything! Well, if you want, you can block out some time on your schedule to work on a particular *task*. This will prevent yourself and others from scheduling you into conflicting meetings or appointments that prevent you from getting the task done.

⚠️ **WARNING**
If the task you wish to schedule time for is not displayed in the *TaskPad*, you can drag it from the **Tasks list** onto the **Calendar icon** in the **Outlook bar**.

✅ **I Need More Time!**
For a big project, you might want to schedule time at regular intervals to work on it. See Part 3, Task 8 for help.

Task 7: Scheduling Time for a Task

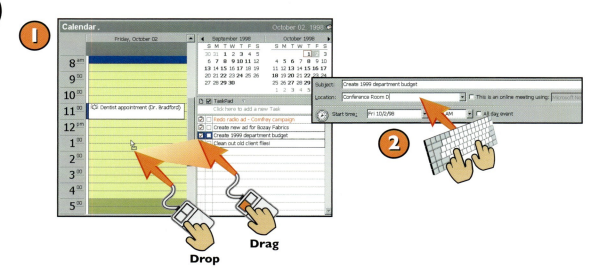

Drop Drag

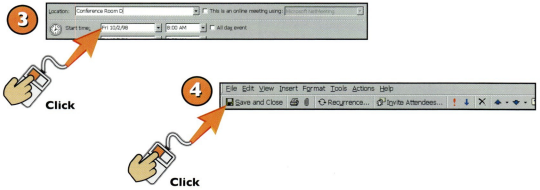

Click

Click

1 Drag the task you wish to schedule and drop it in the appointment area.

2 Type a **Location** if applicable.

3 Adjust the **Start time** and **End time** if needed.

4 Click **Save and Close**.

Task 8: Scheduling a Recurring Appointment, Meeting, or Event

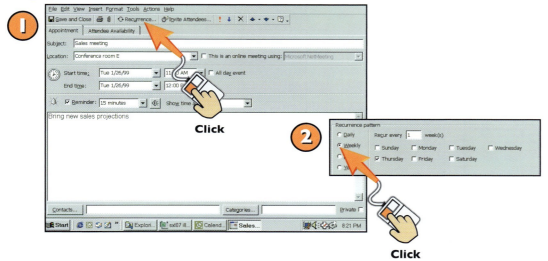

Click

Click

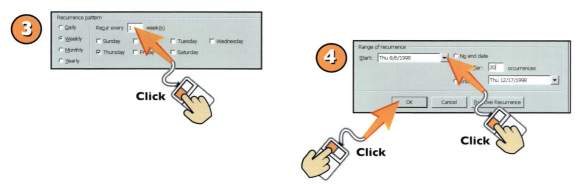

Click

Click

Click

Some appointments, meetings, or events recur at regular intervals. For example, you might attend a sales meeting every Monday, or a parent-teacher conference on the last Friday of each month. Reoccurring activities can be easily scheduled in the Calendar, without having to copy them from one day to another manually.

Could You Repeat That?
Follow these steps to change an existing item so that it recurs. If you know that the appointment or meeting will reoccur at the time you're creating it, you can select **New Recurring Appointment** or **New Recurring Meeting** from the **Actions** menu.

WARNING
If you change a reoccurring appointment/meeting/event later, you'll be asked if you want to change just that occurrence or the entire series.

1 In the appointment, meeting, or event window, click **Recurrence.**

2 Select a recurrence pattern, such as **Weekly**.

3 Select from the additional options that appear.

4 Select a limit for the recurrence in the **Range of recurrence** area and click **OK**.

Task 9: Responding to a Meeting Request

Obviously, if someone sends you a request for a meeting (which comes in the form of an email message), you need to respond. When you respond, you can accept the invitation, reject it, or accept it tentatively. When you accept an invitation to attend a meeting, it's automatically added to your Calendar.

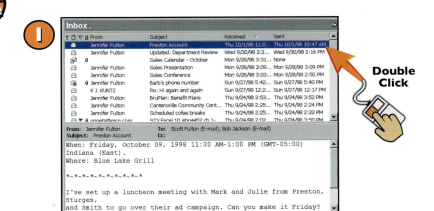

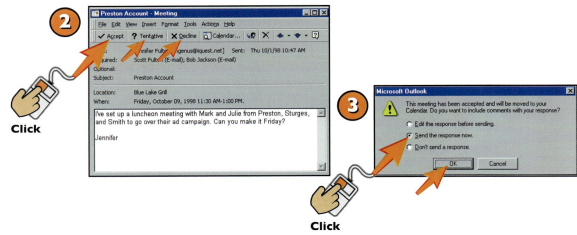

Click

Click

✓ **Put Calendar on AutoPilot**
If you want Calendar to automatically respond to meeting requests from co-workers, see Part 3, Task 10.

✓ **Check Your Schedule**
If you want to check your Calendar before you respond to the meeting request, click the **Calendar** button.

1 Double-click the meeting request to open it.

2 Click either **Accept**, **Tentative**, or **Decline**.

3 Click **Send the response now** and click **OK**.

Task 10: Handling Meeting Requests Automatically

Start Here

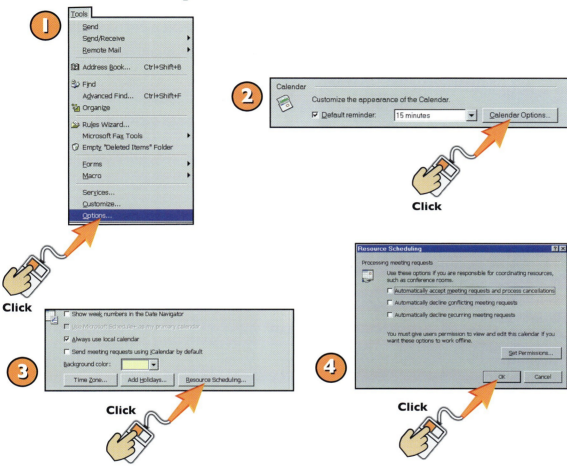

Tools
- Send
- Send/Receive ▶
- Remote Mail ▶
- 📖 Address Book... Ctrl+Shift+B
- 🔍 Find
- Advanced Find... Ctrl+Shift+F
- 🖳 Organize
- 📑 Rules Wizard...
- Microsoft Fax Tools ▶
- 🖲 Empty "Deleted Items" Folder
- Forms ▶
- Macro ▶
- Services...
- Customize...
- Options...

1 Click

Calendar
Customize the appearance of the Calendar.
☑ Default reminder: 15 minutes [Calendar Options...]

2 Click

☐ Show week numbers in the Date Navigator
☐ Use Microsoft Schedule+ as my primary calendar
☑ Always use local calendar
☐ Send meeting requests using iCalendar by default
Background color: [ ]
[Time Zone...] [Add Holidays...] [Resource Scheduling...]

3 Click

Resource Scheduling
Processing meeting requests
Use these options if you are responsible for coordinating resources, such as conference rooms.
☐ Automatically accept meeting requests and process cancellations
☐ Automatically decline conflicting meeting requests
☐ Automatically decline recurring meeting requests
You must give users permission to view and edit this calendar if you want these options to work offline.
[Set Permissions...]
[OK] [Cancel]

4 Click

If you're a part of a large organization, you may find it helpful to have Outlook handle some of your incoming mail—specifically, any requests that you may receive to attend company meetings. Outlook can process the requests and cancellations and automatically accept them, adding or deleting meetings in your Calendar as needed. In addition, Outlook can decline recurring meetings and/or meetings that conflict with other items in your Calendar.

1 Open the **Tools** menu and select **Options**.

2 Click **Calendar Options**.

3 Click **Resource Scheduling**.

4 Select the options you want and click **OK**.

✅ **Delegate Your Calendar**
You can grant *permission* for other people to view, edit, add, and delete items in your Calendar; see Part 3, Task 14 for help.

End Task

Task 11: Canceling a Meeting

If you've arranged a meeting with some colleagues but you've changed your plans, you can easily cancel the meeting. When you cancel a meeting, notices (in the form of email messages) can be sent out so that everyone is made aware of the change.

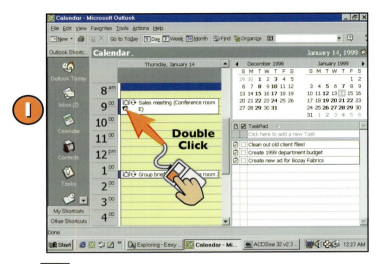

Double Click

✓ **The Meeting's Been Cancelled?**
If you receive a meeting cancellation, just open the email message, and then click **Remove from Calendar** to have Outlook delete the meeting for you.

✓ **Quick Cancel**
To cancel a meeting quickly, you can simply click it to select it, and then press **Delete**.

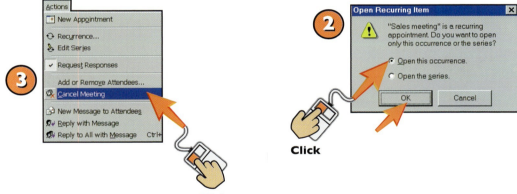

Click

Click

1 Double-click the meeting to open it.

2 If this is a recurring meeting, select **Open this occurrence** or **Open the series** (to delete all occurrences) and click **OK**.

3 Open the **Actions** menu and select **Cancel Meeting**.

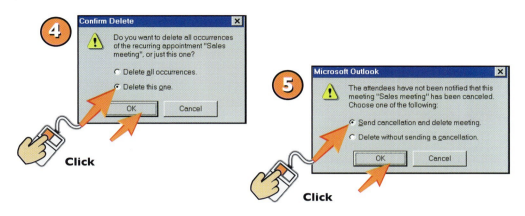

Click

Click

④ Select either **Delete all occurrences** or **Delete this one** and click **OK**.

⑤ Select either **Send cancellation and delete meeting** or **Delete without sending a cancellation** and click **OK**.

⑥ Click **Send** to send the cancellation notices.

✓ **But I Just Want to Change the Meeting Time!**
If you need to simply change the time or location for the meeting, you don't have to cancel it first—you can just make your changes and send out a notification. See Part 3, Task 12 for help.

After scheduling an activity, you may need to make changes to it. For example, you might need to change the time of the activity or its location. Just keep in mind that Calendar keeps track of the amount of time an activity is scheduled for, so if you change the start time, the end time is automatically adjusted. Also, if you make changes to a meeting, you'll be asked if you want to send out notifications (email messages) to let everyone know about the change.

Task 12: Changing an Appointment, Meeting, or Event

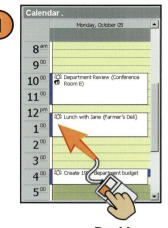

Double Click

Click

✔ **Deleting an Activity**
To delete an activity from the Calendar, click it and then press **Delete**.

✔ **Changing the Date or Time**
You can move an appointment, meeting, or event by simply dragging it onto the Date Navigator and dropping it on the date to which you want to move it. You can also move an activity within the day on which it occurs.

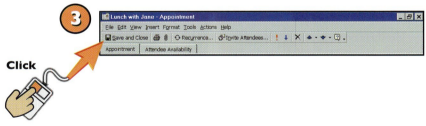

Click

① Double-click the activity you want to change to open it.

② The appointment window appears. Make your changes.

③ Click **Save and Close** to save your changes.

Next Step

Click

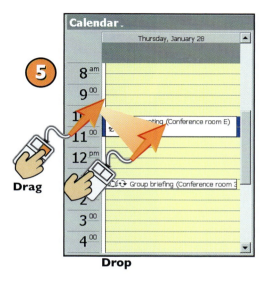

Drag

Drop

4 If you want to change the time for an appointment or meeting, click it.

5 Drag the item to its new time slot, and release the mouse button.

6 You can change the date of an event by dragging it onto a different date on the Date Navigator.

✔ **More Time**
To increase (or decrease) the amount of time an appointment or meeting takes, drag the border of the item to expand it (or shrink it).

End Task

Task 13: Adding Holidays

Including Typical Holidays in Your Calendar

When you first start using the Calendar, national holidays such as Thanksgiving do not automatically appear. You can add holidays yourself by simply adding an event and making it reoccurring, but that's a lot of trouble. Instead, you can have Outlook automatically update your Calendar with its list of holidays.

Start Here

Click

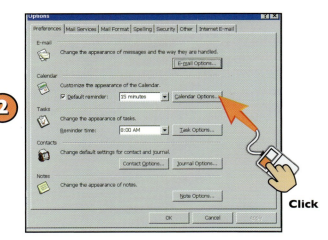

Click

Click

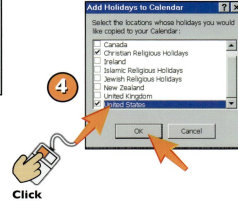

Click

✓ Travel Often?
Holidays are grouped by country, so if you travel a lot, you can add the holidays for more than one country to your Calendar. Just select more than one country in step 4.

1 Open the **Tools** menu and select **Options**.

2 Click **Calendar Options.**

3 Click **Add Holidays**.

4 Select the country and/or religion whose holidays you want to add and click **OK**.

Next Step

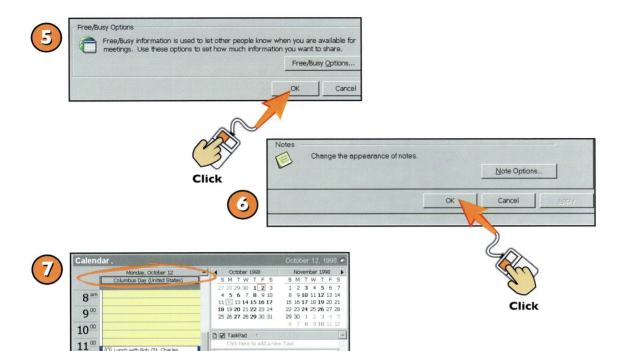

Click

Click

⑤ Click **OK** to return to the Options dialog box.

⑥ Click **OK** to return to the Calendar.

⑦ Holidays appear as events at the top of the appointment area.

WARNING
Holidays appear as events in your Calendar—they do not affect your available time. If you have the day off, double-click the holiday banner and select **Busy or Out of Office** from the **Show time as** drop-down list.

WARNING
If you need to, you can delete a holiday as you would any other event: click it and then press **Delete**.

Task 14: Sharing Your Calendar

If you're part of a large organization, you may want to share your calendar so others can see when you'll be in or out of the office. You can grant higher levels of access if you want, such as allowing an assistant to make additions, changes, and deletions to your Calendar for you.

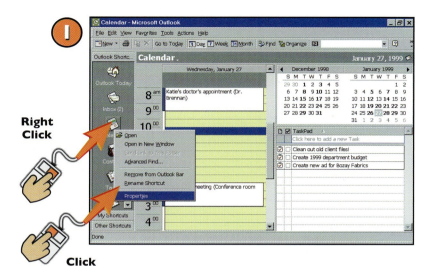

Right Click

Click

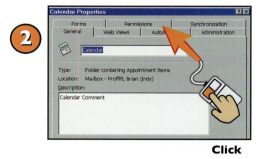

Click

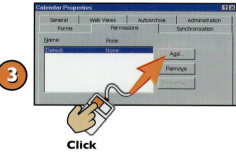

Click

⚠️ **WARNING**
Your company must use Microsoft Exchange Server as its email server for you to perform this task.

✅ **Make Someone Your Assistant**
If you want to grant someone permission to view, create, change, and delete items in your Calendar, select **Editor** from the **Roles** list in step 6.

1 Right-click the **Calendar** *folder* and select **Properties**.

2 Click the **Permissions** tab.

3 Click **Add**.

Next Step

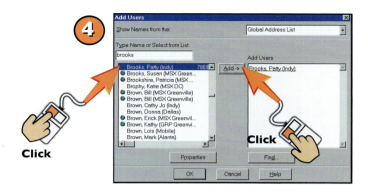

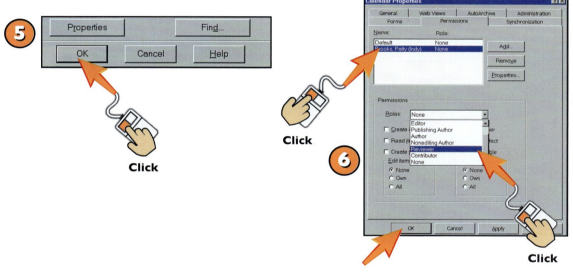

Click

Click

Click

Click

Click

4 Select the person you want to grant access to and click **Add**.

5 Click **OK**.

6 Select the person in the **Name** list, and then select **Reviewer** from the **Roles** list. Click **OK**.

 Net Calendar?
You can also grant access to your Calendar through the *Internet* (or a company *intranet*). See Part 7, Task 13 for help.

Task 15: Printing Your Calendar

Outlook makes it easy to print out your Calendar so you can take it with you when you plan to be out of the office. And if you use a day planner, you can easily adjust the printout to fit your planner exactly by selecting the paper size and paper type you need from the Page Setup dialog box.

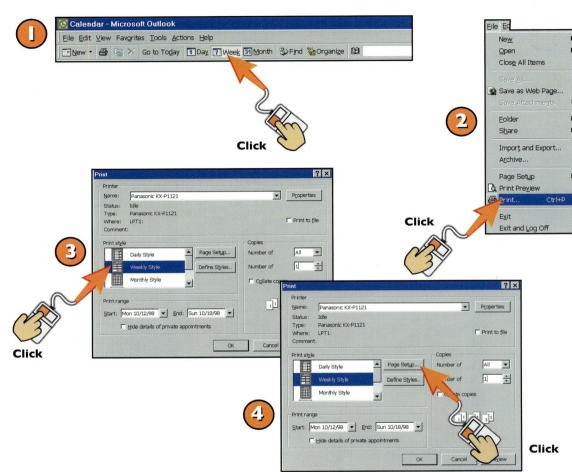

Click

Click

Click

Click

✅ **Selected Days**

To print selected days, press **Ctrl** and click the days you want in the Date Navigator. If the days are consecutive, you can drag over them instead.

✅ **The Quickest Way to Print**

Once you've got your printout looking the way you like, the next time you want to print your Calendar, just select the days you want and click the **Print** button.

1 Click a view button to display the day, week, or month you wish to print.

2 Open the **File** menu and select **Print**.

3 Adjust the **Print style** if needed. For example, to print each day separately, select **Daily Style**.

4 Click **Page Setup**.

Next Step

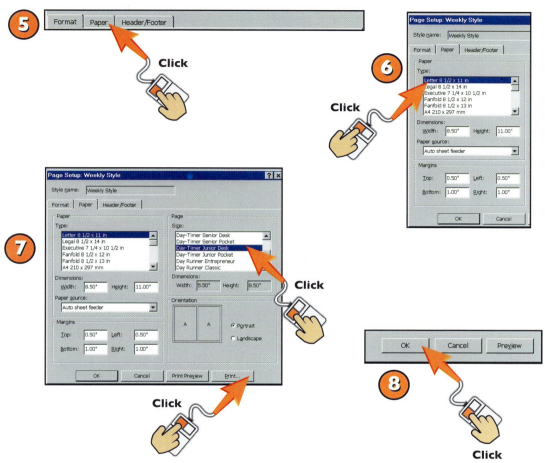

Click

5 Click the **Paper** tab.

6 Select a paper size from the **Paper Type** list.

7 Select a layout from the **Page Size** list and click **Print**.

8 Click **OK** to print your Calendar.

✓ **Preview it First**
You may want to click **Print Preview** in step 7 to preview the Calendar before you print it. That way, you can easily return to the Page Setup dialog box and make any necessary changes.

End Task

Managing Your Contacts

The Contact *folder* helps you organize phone numbers, addresses, *fax* numbers, mobile phone numbers, pager numbers, *email* addresses and other information about the important people in your life, both personal and business.

After information is entered into the **Contacts** list, you can use it to send email messages, schedule an **appointment**, arrange a **meeting**, **delegate** a **task**, visit a client's Web page, and even dial the phone to call a contact.

Tasks

Task 1: Importing a Previous Address List

One of the best features about the Contacts list is that if you've been using another organizer such as **Lotus Organizer** or **Schedule+**, you can easily import that information into Outlook without having to retype it. Outlook supports: **Schedule+, Microsoft Exchange, ACT!, ECCO, Sidekick, Lotus Organizer, Microsoft Mail, Microsoft Access, Microsoft Excel, FoxPro, and dBASE** (all versions). In addition, Outlook supports **.CSV** and **.TXT** files.

✓ **But I Used to Use an Internet Mail Program!**
Outlook also lets you import addresses from your old *Internet* mail program, such as Eudora Pro, Netscape Messenger, *Internet Explorer* Mail, and *Outlook Express*. Just select **Import Internet Mail and Addresses** in step 2.

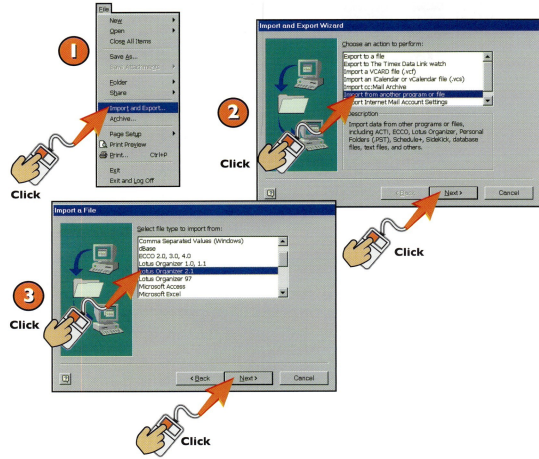

1 Open the **File** menu and select **Import and Export**.

2 Click **Import from another program or file**. Then click **Next>**.

3 Select your program name in the **Select file type to import from** list. Then click **Next>**. If you see a message telling you to install the feature, click **Yes**.

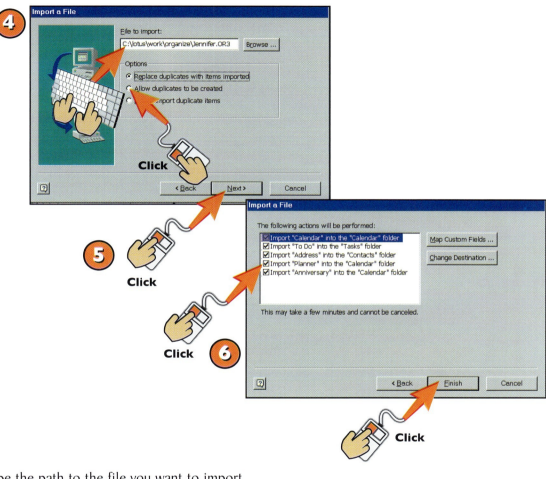

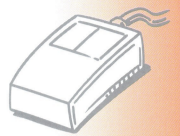

4 Type the path to the file you want to import.

5 Choose how you want duplicate entries handled. Click **Next**.

6 Click the actions you want taken and click **Finish**.

Everyone has important people in their life—both business and personal. With the Contacts list, you can keep track of them easily. You'll find fields for name, address (business and home), phone number, fax number, email address, Web page address, and more.

✓ **New Guy, Same Old Company**
Need to add a new contact for the same company as an existing contact? See Part 4, Task 3 for help.

✓ **Make It Your Own**
You can customize the fields on the General tab by selecting the ones you want to use. Just click the **down** arrow next to a field name you don't intend to use (such as the Mobile phone number) and select the type of field you want to use. Or, double-up! Just enter the information in a standard field, such as **Business Address**, and then select another field using the **down** arrow, such as **Home Address**. Both fields are stored, but only one is displayed.

Task 2: Adding a Contact

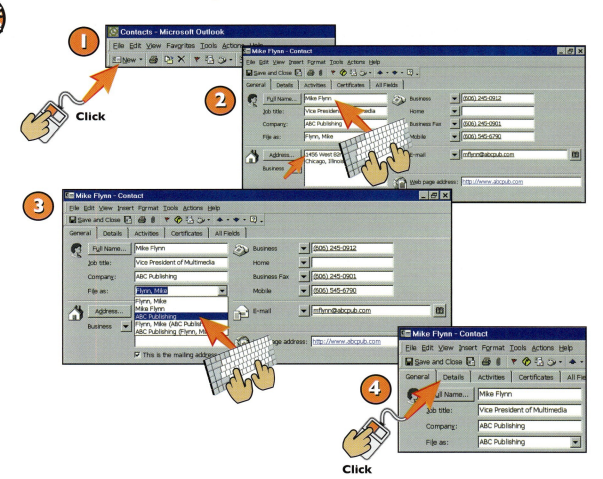

Click

Click

1. Click the **New Contact** button.

2. Enter the contact's **Full Name**. Enter additional information in the appropriate fields.

3. From the **File As** list, select the text you wish to use to sort this entry in the Contacts list.

4. Click the **Details** tab.

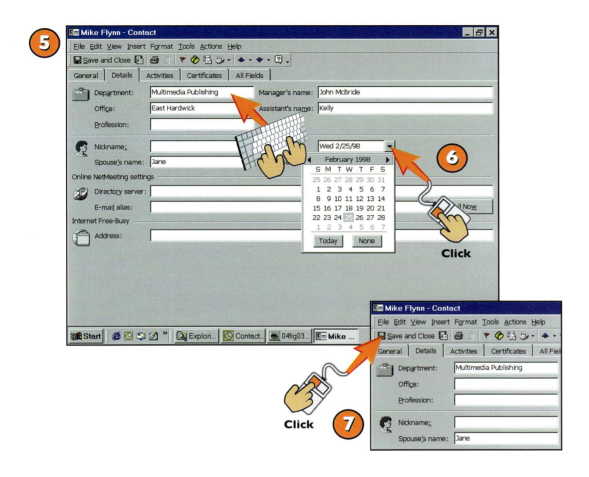

5 Enter additional information about a contact, such as his department name, assistant's name, spouse's name, and so on.

6 To enter a date, click the **down** arrow and select the date you want.

7 Click **Save and Close**.

✔ **Create a Contact from His or Her Email**
You can create a new contact from an email *message* by simply dragging that message onto the **Contact** icon on the *Outlook bar*.

❗ **WARNING!**
If you need to enter some kind of unique information for a contact, click the **All Fields** tab, and then choose **All Contact fields** from the **Select from** list. If you don't find what you need there, create a new field by clicking **New,** entering a name for the field, and clicking **OK**.

When two people work for the same company, a lot of their contact information is usually the same: the company name (of course), business address, and phone and fax numbers. When you create a new contact based on an existing contact from the same company, this basic information is copied to the new contact's record—eliminating the need to retype it all.

Task 3: Adding Another Contact from the Same Company

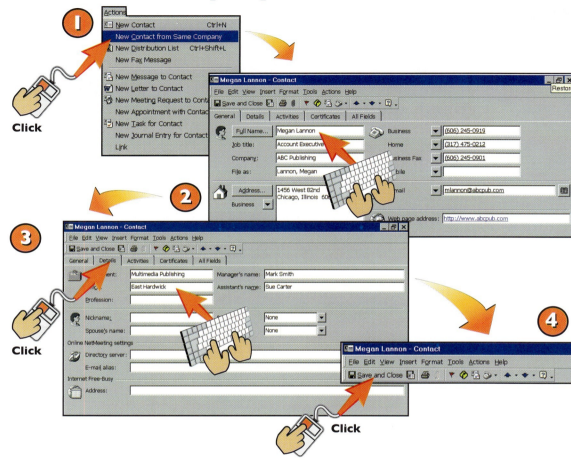

Start Here

Click

Click

Click

⚠ **WARNING!**
The fields that are copied to the new entry include: company name, business address, business phone, business fax, and company main phone (if entered on the All Fields tab). Other fields, such as the Web site address, are not copied.

① Select the contact you wish to copy, and then open the **Actions** menu and select **New Contact from Same Company**.

② Enter the contact's **Full Name** and other information as needed.

③ Click the **Details** tab and enter any additional information you have.

④ Click **Save and Close**.

End Task

Task 4: Changing Contact Information

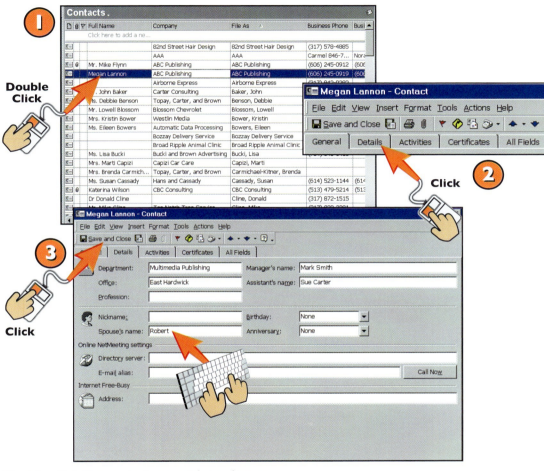

Double Click

Click

Click

You may have to change a contact's information for many reasons: the contact's title and position may change, his company might relocate, or his phone number might change. Instead of changing existing data for a contact, you may want to add new information. For example, you might have just found out what your contact's assistant's name is, and now you want to enter it. Adding and changing information for a contact follows a similar process.

✔️ **Changing What You See**
To change a field that is visible (such as the contact's business phone number), just click in that field. Press **Backspace** to delete characters to the left of the cursor, or **Delete** to remove characters to the right. Then type your entry. When you're through, press **Enter**.

① Double-click the contact you wish to change.

② If needed, click the tab that contains the field you want to change.

③ Make your changes, and then click **Save and Close** to save them.

Task 5: Creating a Distribution List

Start Here

If you often send email messages to the same small group of people, you should create a personal *distribution list.* Then, instead of selecting each individual person's name to send the message, you simply select the distribution list you created. The names in the list are used to send copies of the message to multiple people.

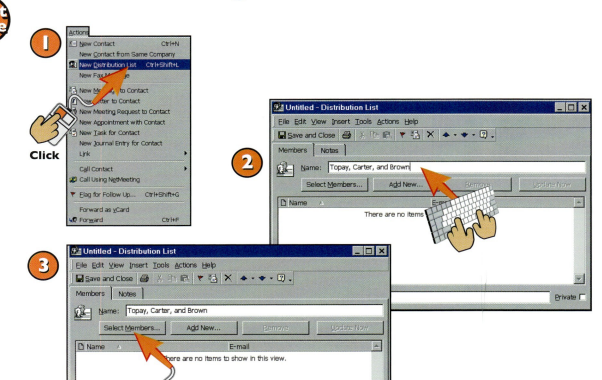

✓ **More Than One**
You can create multiple distribution lists if needed. For example, you might need a distribution list for everyone in your department and another one for your fellow managers.

⚠ **WARNING**
Before you create your distribution list, the contacts you want to include must already exist and have email addresses.

1 Open the **Actions** menu and select **New Distribution List**.

2 Type a name for your **Distribution List**.

3 Click **Select Members**.

Next Step

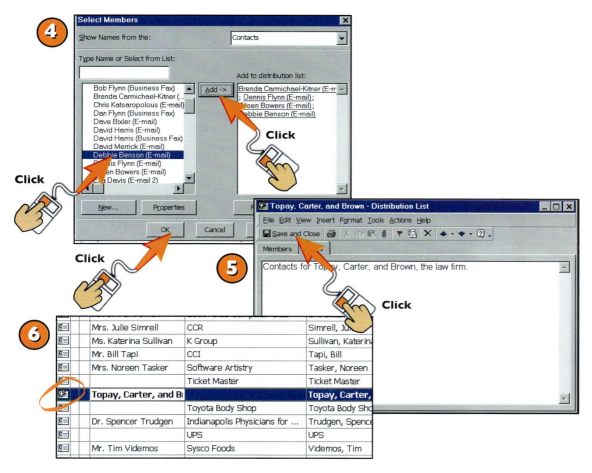

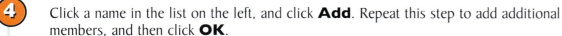

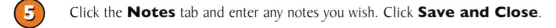

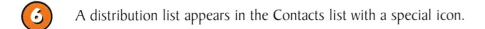

4 Click a name in the list on the left, and click **Add**. Repeat this step to add additional members, and then click **OK**.

5 Click the **Notes** tab and enter any notes you wish. Click **Save and Close**.

6 A distribution list appears in the Contacts list with a special icon.

✓ **Sending Messages Using the Distribution List**
To send the same email message to everyone on your distribution list, simply click the distribution list you want to use, click the **New Message to Contact** button, and create your message as usual.

End Task

If you make a number of phone calls during the day, the process can be quite annoying and repetitive. Because you have to open Outlook to look up the number, why not have it dial the phone for you? (For help in logging incoming calls, see Part 6, Task 4.)

✓ **One Phone Line**
For Outlook to dial your phone, you must be using the same phone line for both your phone and *modem*.

⚠ **WARNING!**
If you normally dial a **9** to get an outside line, you may want to verify that this option has been set up properly. Click **Dialing Properties**, and check the information in the **When dialing from here** section.

Task 6: Phoning a Contact

Start Here

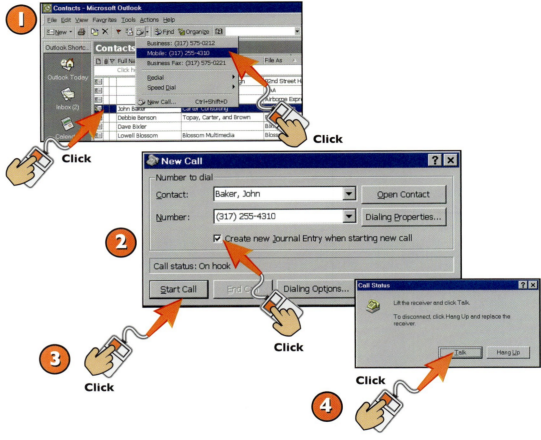

① Click the name of the contact you want to call, click the arrow on the **AutoDialer** button, and then click the phone number you wish to dial.

② To log the call, click **Create new Journal Entry when starting new call**.

③ Click **Start Call**.

④ The modem dials the number. Lift the receiver and click **Talk**.

Next Step

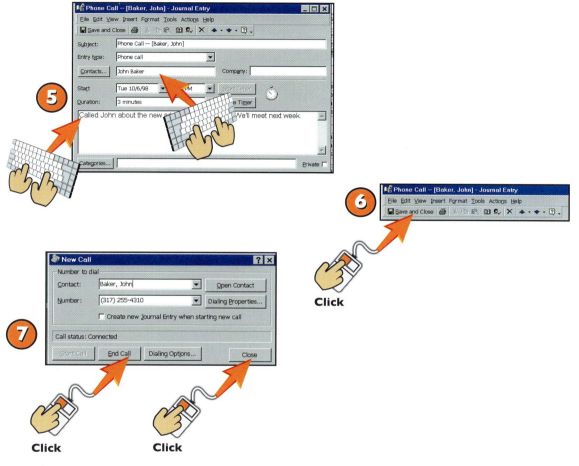

Click

Click   **Click**

5 Type the contact's name in the **Contacts** box. Type your notes into the large text box.

6 Hang up the receiver and click **Save and Close**.

7 Click **End Call**. Then click **Close** to return to Outlook.

✓ **Speed, Too**
You can save numbers you dial frequently in a *Speed Dial list*, which makes them easier to access. See Part 4, Tasks 7 and 8.

✓ **Dear Diary**
If you logged the call in the *Journal*, you can view the entry by double-clicking a contact, and then clicking the **Activities** tab.

End Task

In Part 4, Task 6, you learned to have Outlook dial a contact's number for you. If there are particular people you dial frequently, you can add their phone numbers to the Speed Dial list. Then you can dial their phone numbers quickly (see Part 4, Task 8 for help).

Task 7: Creating a Speed Dial List

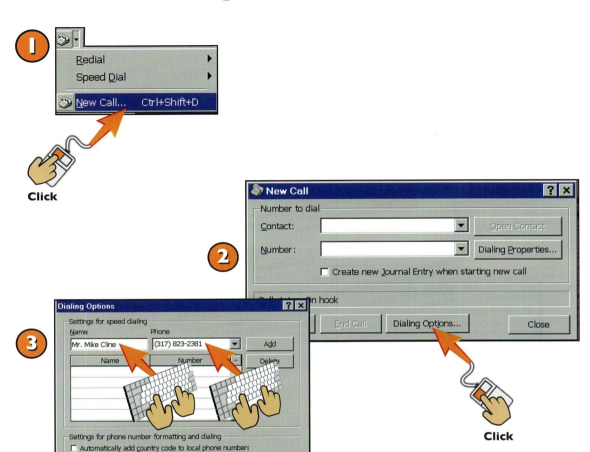

✓ **Calling Someone You Want to Speed Dial?** You can also perform this task from the New Call dialog box, just before or just after you make a call.

① Click the arrow on the **AutoDialer** button and select **New Call**.

② Click **Dialing Options**.

③ Type the **Name** of the person whose number you wish to add.

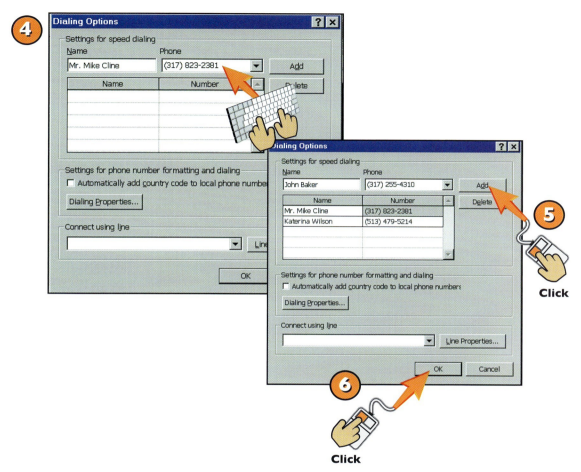

Click

Click

4 Type his or her **Phone** number if it does not appear when you press **Tab**.

5 Click **Add**.

6 Repeat steps 3, 4, and 5 to add additional numbers. When you're through, click **OK**.

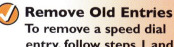

Remove Old Entries
To remove a speed dial
entry, follow steps 1 and 2,
select the entry you want
to delete, and click **Delete**.

Task 8: Calling a Speed Dial Number

Speed dialing with Outlook is similar to using the speed dial buttons on your phone. In Part 4, Task 7, you learned how to add numbers you dial frequently to the Speed Dial list. In this task, you'll learn how to use the Speed Dial list to dial a number without having to look up the contact first.

Start Here

Click

Click

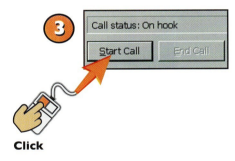
Click

Click

⚠ WARNING!
For Outlook to dial your phone, you must be using the same phone line for both your phone and modem.

✅ Saving a Record of Activities
If you create a Journal entry of the call, you can view it later by double-clicking the contact, and then clicking the **Activities** tab.

① Click the arrow on the **AutoDialer** button, select **Speed Dial**, and then select the number you want to call.

② To log the call, click **Create new Journal Entry when starting new call**.

③ Click **Start Call**.

④ The modem dials the number. Lift the receiver and click **Talk**.

Next Step

Click

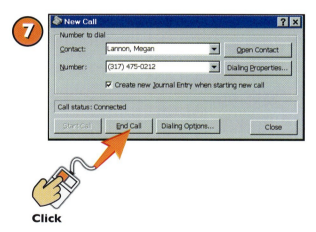

Click

5 Type the contact's name in the **Contacts** box. Type your notes into the large text box.

6 Hang up the receiver and click **Save and Close**.

7 Click **End Call**. Then click **Close** to return to Outlook.

Task 9: Sending a Message to a Contact

In Part 2, Task 1, you learned how to create an email message from the *Inbox* folder. Luckily, even though you might be working in the Contacts folder, Outlook makes it easy to send any messages you need.

Start Here

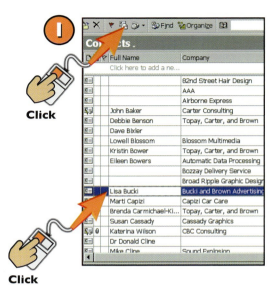

Click

Click

Click

✓ **Alternate Method**
You can also perform this task while viewing contact information in the Contact window.

✓ **Quick Create?**
Another way to create an email message is to drag a contact name onto the Inbox icon in the Outlook bar.

Click

1 Select the contact to whom you wish to send a message and click **New Message to Contact**.

2 Type a **Subject** and the text of your message.

3 Click **Send**.

End Task

Start Here

Task 10: Scheduling an Appointment with a Contact

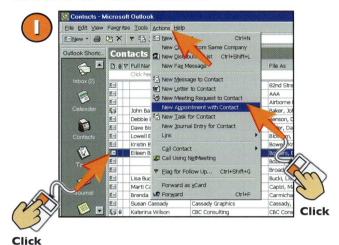

①

Click

Click

In Part 3, Task 3, you learned how to create an appointment, and in Part 3, Task 4, you learned how to associate a contact name with that appointment. Here you'll learn the easiest way to perform both tasks at the same time. By the way, if you would like to send your contact an email message to confirm the appointment, create a meeting instead. See Part 4, Task 11 for help.

②

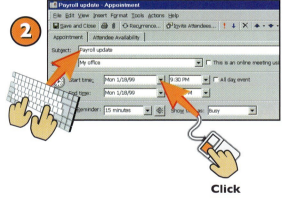

③

Click

Click

✓ A Good Association
When a contact is associated with an appointment in the *Calendar*, you can look up that contact's information more easily. Just open the appointment and double-click the contact's name that appears at the bottom of the window.

① Select the contact with whom you wish to meet, open the **Actions** menu, and select **New Appointment with Contact**.

② Type a **Subject and Location**, and select a **Start** and **End Time**. Set additional options as needed.

③ Click **Save and Close**.

End Task

In Part 4, Task 10, you learned how to create an appointment and associate it with a contact. Here, you'll learn how to set up a meeting instead. This allows you to invite multiple people from your Contacts list and to send out email messages that confirm the *event* for each participant.

ⓘ WARNING!

If you set up a meeting with someone who is not connected to your company's *network*, an email message will be sent, but the contact will not be able to confirm his participation as described in Part 3, Task 9, *even if he also uses Outlook*. He can, however, *reply* to your message as he might to any other.

✔ Get Creative

Another way to create a meeting is to drag a contact name onto the Calendar icon in the Outlook bar.

Task 11: Scheduling a Meeting with a Contact

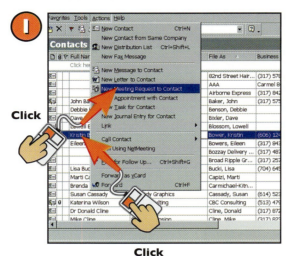

Click

Click

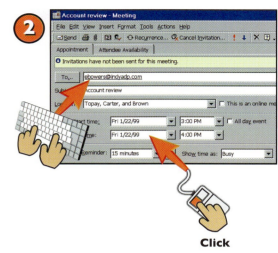

Click

Click

Click

① Select the contact with whom you wish to meet, open the **Actions** menu, and select **New Meeting Request to Contact**.

② Type a **Subject and Location**, and select a **Start** and **End Time**. Set additional options as needed.

③ Click the **Attendee Availability** tab.

④ Click **Invite Others**.

Next Step

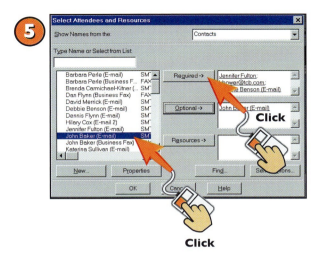

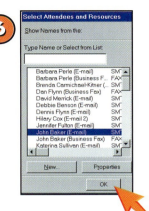

Click

Click

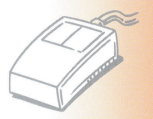

Click

Click

5 Select a name from the list and click either the **Required** or the **Optional** button.

6 Repeat to invite additional people, and then click **OK**.

7 Click **Send**. Invitations in the form of email messages are sent to each person listed.

WARNING!
A contact's schedule will
not display in the Meeting
Planner unless that contact
is also connected to your
company's network.

Let AutoPick Decide
If most of the contacts
invited to this meeting are
connected to your
company network (and
thus their schedules are
visible), click **AutoPick** to
let it find the first available
time slot in everyone's
schedules.

Task 12: Creating a Task Associated with a Contact

One reason for associating a task with a particular contact is to keep track of the amount of work you do for that contact. If your company bills by the hour, this is a handy feature. Even if it doesn't, you can use this task to keep important contact information close at hand while you're working on an important project.

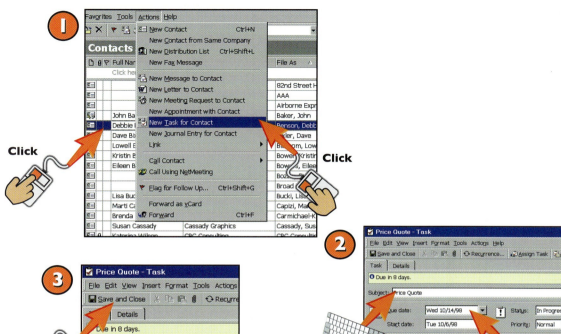

Start Here

Click

Click

Click

Click

✓ No Guilt in This Association

After you associate a task with a contact, you can view the contact's information quickly by opening the task and double-clicking the contact name that appears at the bottom of the window.

✓ More Info?

If you need more information on how to create a task, see Part 5, Task 1 for help.

1 Select the contact for whom you are performing this task, open the **Actions** menu, and select **New Task for Contact.**

2 Type a description for the task. Set a **Due date, Start date, Priority,** and other options as needed.

3 Click **Save and Close**.

End Task

Task 13: Visiting a Contact's World Wide Web Page

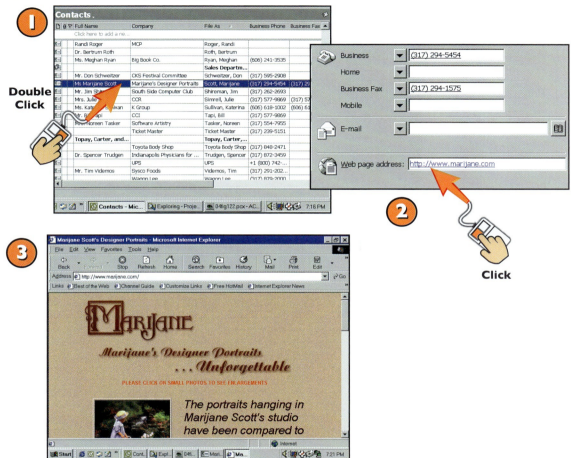

Double Click

Click

2

3

One field you can enter for a contact is his or her World Wide Web page. With many companies (and individuals) creating a presence on the Internet, keeping up with the information made available there is becoming more and more important. With Outlook, you can visit a contact's Web page quickly and easily.

1 Double-click the contact whose Web page you would like to visit.

2 Click the link to the Contacts Web page.

3 The Web page appears in your Web browser.

 **WARNING!**
For Outlook to connect to a contact's Web page, you must have a *Web browser* installed and a connection to the Internet.

 End Task

Through your connection to the Internet, Outlook (with a little help from Microsoft's Expedia Maps) can locate any address you specify and display a map to that location in your Web browser. You might find this helpful if you need to drive to a client's location (or a friend's house) for the first time. You can even print out the map and take it with you.

WARNING!
For Outlook to display a map to a contact's address, you must have a Web browser installed and a connection to the Internet.

Not Found?
If Expedia Maps can not locate the address, you'll be taken to a page where you can enter more information, such as a nearby cross street.

Task 14: Viewing a Contact's Address on a Map

Start Here

Double Click

Click

1   Double-click the contact whose address you wish to view.

2   Click **Display Map of Address**.

3   A map of the address appears in your Web browser.

End Task

Task 15: Looking Up Associated Contact Information

Start Here

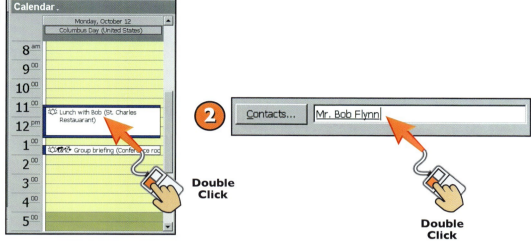

Double Click

Double Click

In Part 4, Tasks 10–12, you learned how to create an appointment, meeting, or task for a contact. Once an Outlook item is associated (linked) to someone in your Contacts list, you can easily pull up his or her information when needed. For example, suppose you're getting ready for an appointment and you need to look up the contact's address or phone number. Outlook makes this easy to do.

① Double-click the Calendar, **Tasks**, Journal, or Notes item whose contact information you wish to view.

② Double-click the contact name.

③ The Contact window appears.

✔ **Quick Association**
If you didn't associate a contact with an item when you created it, you can do so after the fact. See Part 4, Task 17 for help.

⚠ **WARNING!**
To view contact information associated with an email message, just double-click the message to open it, right-click the *sender's* name, and select **Look up Contact**.

End Task

With the help of the Journal (which you'll learn more about in Part 6), you can automatically keep track of office activity, such as the creation of an Excel worksheet. This makes the file quickly available from within Outlook. You can link non-Outlook files to a contact also. For example, if you've created a graphic image for a new ad campaign, a sales worksheet, or a ten page report, you can associate the file with a name in your Contacts list. Once a file (any file) is linked to a contact, you can locate and open it quickly by using Outlook.

✓ **Automatic Association**
You can associate Office 2000 items (such as a Word *document* or an Excel worksheet) with a contact automatically. See Part 4, Task 1 for help.

Task 16: Linking a Document to a Contact Name

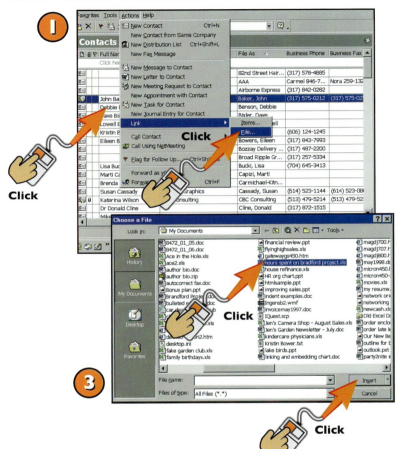

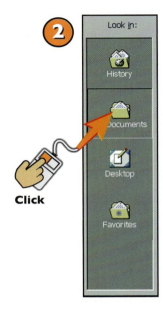

1. Select a contact, open the **Actions** menu, select **Link**, and select **File**.

2. Change to the folder that contains the file you wish to *link*.

3. Click the file, and then click **Insert**.

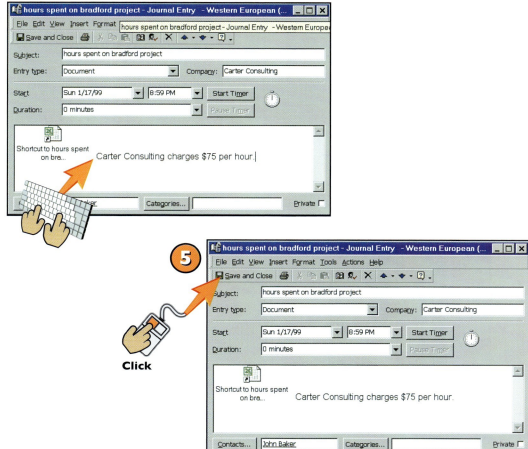

Click

4 Type your notes (if any) in the large text box.

5 Click **Save and Close**.

 Viewing the Associated File
After a file is linked to a contact, you can open it when needed from Outlook. See Part 6, Task 2 for help.

Task 17: Linking Multiple Outlook Items to a Contact Name

Start Here

Although you can associate a single appointment, meeting, task, or note with a contact when you create it, you may wish to add some history to a contact by going back to prior activities and associating them to a contact in one simple step.

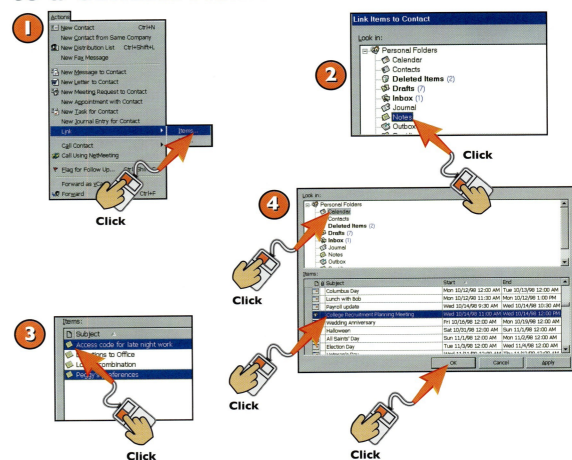

Click

Click

Click

Click

Click

Click

✅ Viewing an Associated Item
After an item is linked to a contact, you can quickly view it when needed. See Part 6, Task 2 for help.

✅ Do Nothing
You do not need to do anything for Outlook to automatically track email related activity with a contact, such as incoming or outgoing email messages, meeting requests, or task requests.

1 Select a contact, open the **Actions** menu, select **Link**, and select **Items**.

2 Click the folder that contains the item(s) you wish to link.

3 Press **Ctrl**, and click as many items as you like, and then click **Apply**.

4 Click another folder and select additional items if you want. Click **OK**.

End Task

Task 18: Sending a Contact's vCard with an Email Message

Click

Click

Click

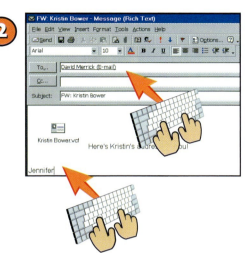

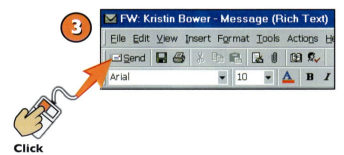

Click

1 Select a contact, open the **Actions** menu, and select **Forward as vCard**.

2 Type an address in the **To** text box. Type a note if you like.

3 Click **Send**.

A *vCard*, or virtual business card, is just what it sounds like: a file that contains contact information. You can share a contact's address, phone number, and so on with a colleague through vCards, which you can easily attach to an outgoing message. To use the vCard, your friend must use Outlook, Outlook Express, Internet Mail, Netscape Messenger, or some email program that's compatible.

✓ Saving a vCard You Get
If someone sends you a vCard in an email message, just drag the vCard icon onto the Contacts icon in the Outlook bar.

! WARNING!
If your colleague does not use a compatible email program, you can save a contact's information as text using the **File, Save As** command, and include the file in a message.

Task 19: Sharing Your Contacts List

Allowing Others to View Your Contacts

In Part 2, Task 36, you learned how to share your Inbox with others in your organization. Part 3, Task 14, showed you how to share your Calendar as well. If you're part of a large company, sharing information is critical—especially if you're hard to reach. In this task, you'll learn how to allow viewing-only access to the Contacts list. However, you can grant higher levels of access if you wish, such as allowing an assistant or members of your department to make additions, changes, and deletions to the Contacts list on your behalf.

Start Here

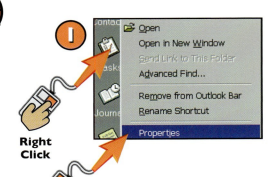

Right Click

Click

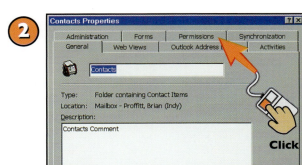

Click

Click

⚠️ **WARNING**
Your company must use Microsoft Exchange Server as its email server for you to perform this task.

1 Right-click the **Contacts** folder and select **Properties**.

2 Click the **Permissions** tab.

3 Click **Add**.

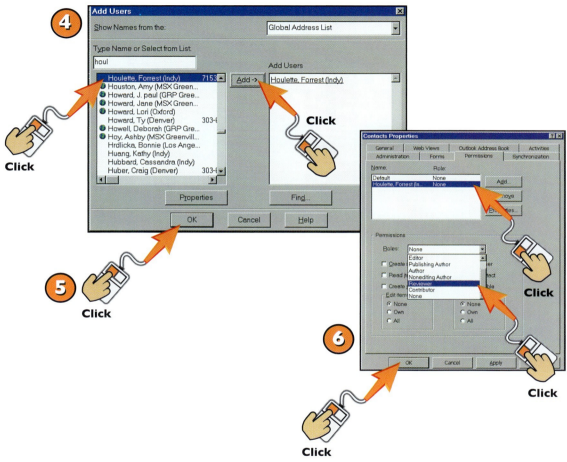

Internet Contacts?
You can also grant access to your Contacts list through the Internet (or a company *intranet*). See Part 7, Task 8 for more information.

4 Select the person you want to grant access to and click **Add**.

5 Click **OK**.

6 Select the person in the Names list, and then select **Reviewer** from the **Roles** list. Click **OK**.

Make Someone Your Assistant
If you want to grant someone *permission* to view, create, change, and delete items in your Contacts list, select **Editor** from the **Roles** list in step 6.

End Task

Task 20: Creating a Letter to a Contact with Word

When you need to send some correspondence to a contact, why not let Outlook help you? With the help of Microsoft Word, you can create a professional looking letter, complete with the contact's name and address and your own as well. Word lets you choose from several letter styles and options so you can get the exact look you want in minutes—and the process couldn't be easier.

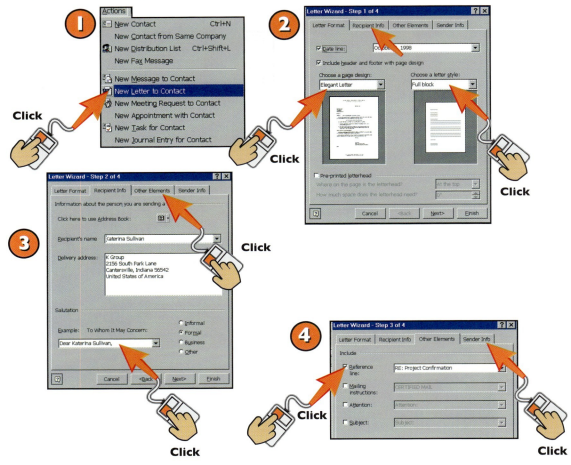

Start Here

Actions

New Contact	Ctrl+N
New Contact from Same Company	
New Distribution List	Ctrl+Shift+L
New Fax Message	
New Message to Contact	
New Letter to Contact	
New Meeting Request to Contact	
New Appointment with Contact	
New Task for Contact	
New Journal Entry for Contact	

Click

Letter Wizard - Step 1 of 4

Letter Format | Recipient Info | Other Elements | Sender Info

☑ Date line: October, 1998

☑ Include header and footer with page design

Choose a page design: Elegant Letter

Choose a letter style: Full block

☐ Pre-printed letterhead

Where on the page is the letterhead? At the top

How much space does the letterhead need? 0"

Cancel | <Back | Next> | Finish

Click **Click** **Click**

Letter Wizard - Step 2 of 4

Letter Format | Recipient Info | Other Elements | Sender Info

Information about the person you are sending a

Click here to use Address Book:

Recipient's name Katerina Sullivan

Delivery address: K Group
2156 South Park Lane
Cantersville, Indiana 56542
United States of America

Salutation

Example: To Whom It May Concern:

Dear Katerina Sullivan,

☐ Informal
☑ Formal
☐ Business
☐ Other

Cancel | <Back | Next> | Finish

Click **Click**

Letter Wizard - Step 3 of 4

Letter Format | Recipient Info | Other Elements | Sender Info

Include

☑ Reference line: RE: Project Confirmation

☐ Mailing instructions: CERTIFIED MAIL

☐ Attention: Attention:

☐ Subject: Subject:

Click **Click**

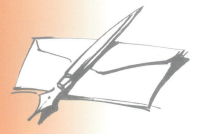

1 Click a contact, open the **Actions** menu, and click **New Letter to Contact**.

2 Select a page design and letter style. Select additional options as needed. Click the **Recipient Info** tab.

3 Verify the address and select a **Salutation**. Click the **Other Elements** tab.

4 Click any elements you want to add to your letter, and then click the **Sender Info** tab.

Next Step

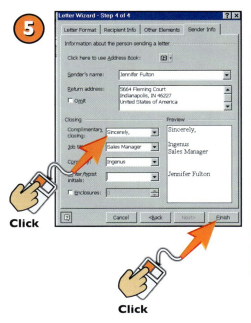

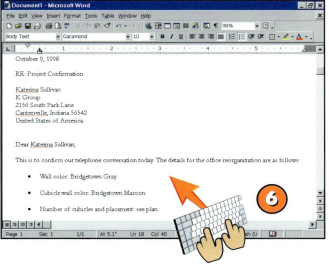

5 Select a **Complimentary closing** and any additional options you wish. Click **Finish**.

6 Type your letter.

7 Click **Print**.

If you need to send the same letter to multiple people, why not combine the best of Outlook and Word to make the job easier? It's simple to perform a mail merge—a merging of your Contacts list with a Word document. When you create the document, you insert merge codes that symbolize the data you want to use from each contact—codes such as title and last_name. When the document is merged with the selected contacts, you get individual copies of the same letter, with the data from each contact inserted in the proper place, as in the salutation, Dear Mr. Flynn.

⚠ WARNING

You must have Microsoft Word installed to perform this task.

Task 21: Creating a Letter to Multiple Contacts

Start Here

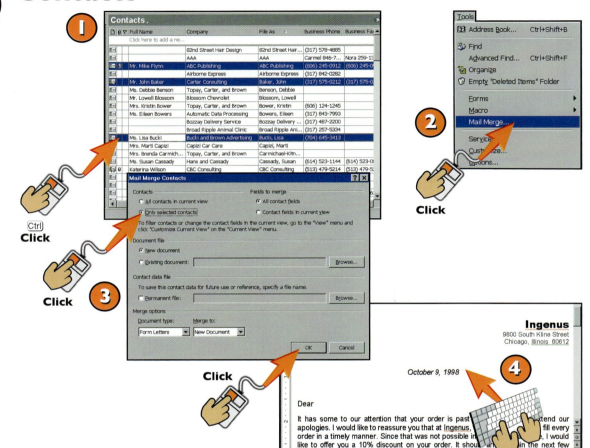

Ctrl Click

Click

Click

Click

Click

Ingenus
9800 South Kline Street
Chicago, Illinois 60612

October 9, 1998

Dear

It has some to our attention that your order is past ... tend our apologies. I would like to reassure you that at Ingenus, ... fill every order in a timely manner. Since that was not possible in ... , I would like to offer you a 10% discount on your order. It shoul ... n the next few

① Press **Ctrl** and click the contacts you want to include.

② Open the **Tools** menu and click **Mail Merge**.

③ Click **Only selected contacts** and click **OK**.

④ Type your document.

Next Step

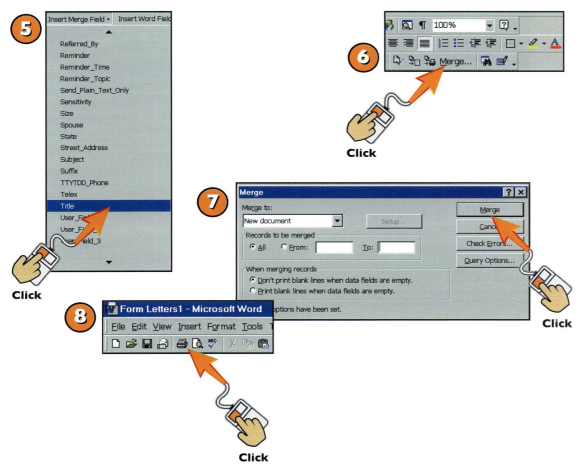

Click

Click

Click

Click

5 To insert a merge field, open the **Insert Merge Field** list and select a Contacts field.

6 When you're finished inserting merge fields, click **Start Mail Merge**.

7 Click **Merge.**

8 Click **Print**.

✓ **Mirror, Mirror**
You can follow this same process to create the same fax, email message, envelope, or mailing label for your contacts.

✓ **Why Not All?**
If you want to send a letter to *all* your contacts, just skip steps 1 and 3.

End Task

Task 22: Printing Your Contact List

If your job takes you out of the office a lot, why not print out your Contacts list so you can take it along? It's easy to do. If you use a day planner, you can adjust the paper size and paper type to fit it.

✓ To Select or Not to Select?

When you select **Table** style (which prints only what's displayed onscreen), all contacts are printed unless you select the ones you want. If you choose **Memo** style (which prints all contact data), *only* the selected contacts are printed. To select contacts, press **Ctrl** and click the contacts you wish to print. To select all contacts, press **Ctrl+A**.

✓ The Quickest Way to Print

Once you've made selections in the Page Setup dialog box to fit your day planner, just click the **Print** button the next time you want to print your Contacts list.

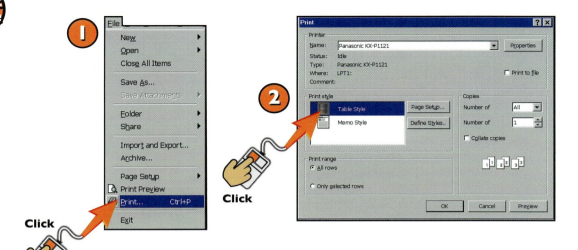

Click

Click

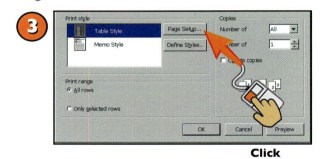

Click

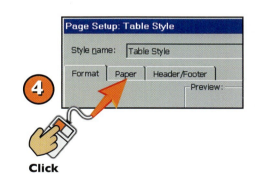

Click

Click

1 Open the **File** menu and select **Print**.

2 Click the **Print style** you want and select the options you desire from the **Print range** area.

3 Click **Page Setup**.

4 Click the **Paper** tab.

Next
Step

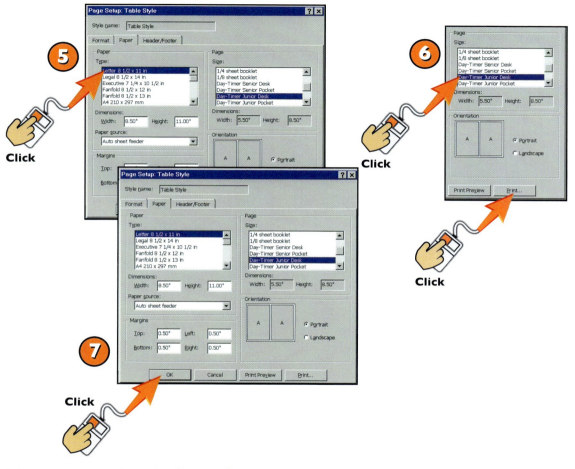

5 Select a paper size from the **Paper Type** list.

6 Select a layout from the **Page Size** list and click **Print**.

7 Click **OK** to print your Contacts list.

✓ **Preview it Before Printing**
You may want to click **Print Preview** in step **6** to preview the Contacts list before you print it. That way, you can easily return to the Page Setup dialog box and make any necessary changes.

✓ **Your Point of View**
Additional print style options may appear in the Print dialog box depending on the view you are using.

End Task

Keeping Track of Things to Do with the Tasks List

Need to complete some performance reviews by next Monday? Need to pick up your dry cleaning on the way home tonight? The **Tasks** list can help you keep track of all the things you need to get done, both business and personal. In the Tasks list, you can enter a task, set a deadline, and even post a **reminder** so you'll remember to complete the **task** on time. You can even set up **recurring** tasks, such as a monthly sales report.

If you're working on a project, the Tasks list can help you track your progress. As you complete each part of the project, you can update the percentage completed. You can even generate **status report**s to update others as to your progress.

When a task is due, it appears in the **Calendar** for that day. As you finish tasks during the day, you can quickly mark them as completed. You can add tasks directly to the **TaskPad** that appears in the Calendar, or you can add them through the Tasks list itself.

Tasks

Task 1: Adding a Task

In addition to helping you keep track of your *appointments*, meetings, colleagues, and friends, Outlook can also help you manage the things you need to get done. As you've probably noticed by now, current tasks are displayed in the Calendar. However, if you wish to see your complete list of tasks (including completed tasks), you must switch to the Tasks *folder*. Here, you'll learn how to add a task while in the Tasks folder. If you want to add a task from the Calendar, see Part 5, Task 2 for help.

Start Here

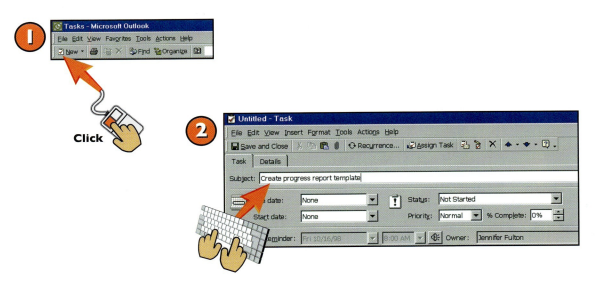

Click

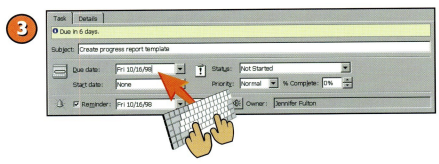

✅ **Fast Task**
To enter a task quickly, type its description in the **Subject** text box at the top of the Tasks list, and then select a date from the **Due Date** list.

✅ **Can You Repeat That?**
For help making this task reoccur at regular intervals, see Part 5, Task 4.

① Click the **New Task** button.

② Type a description for the task in the **Subject** text box.

③ Enter a **Due date**.

Next Step

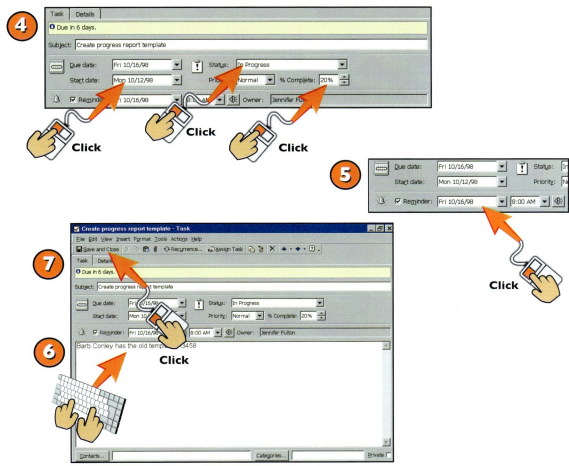

4 If you've already started working on the task, enter a **Start date** and **% Complete**. In addition, select **In Progress** from the **Status** drop-down list.

5 Select the date and time when you want the **Reminder** to go off.

6 Add any notes about the task in the large text box.

7 Click **Save and Close**.

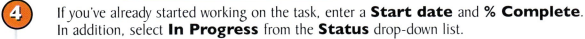

✅ **Let's Get Started!**
The Start date you enter in step 4 can also represent the date on which you'd like to start working on the task.

✅ **Associating a Task**
You can *link* a task with a contact if needed. See Part 5, Task 3 for help. In addition, you can associate a task with a *category* (see Part 7, Task 7).

End Task

Task 2: Using Calendar to Add a Task

In Part 5, Task 1, you learned how to add a task while in the Tasks folder. But if all you want to do is to add a simple task and description, you can do that from within the Calendar folder (on the TaskPad), without having to switch to Tasks. Tasks appear on the TaskPad in alphabetical order. Red tasks are overdue—*a task will not appear before its start date.*

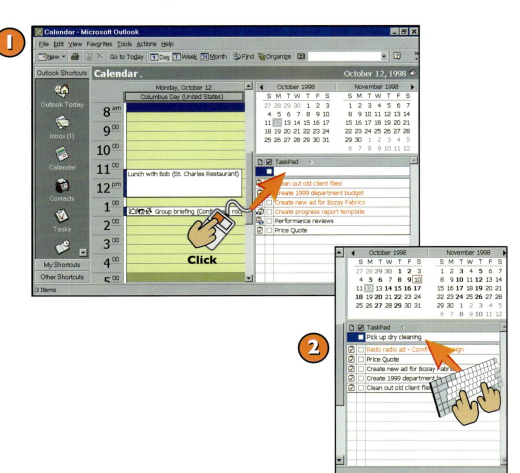

✔ But I Want More!
If you like, you can add a complete task (with due date, start date, and so on) without leaving the Calendar. Just double-click the TaskPad, enter the task data, and click **Save** and **Close.**

1 Click the line at the top of the **TaskPad**.

2 Type a description for the task and press **Enter.**

Task 3: Associating a Contact Name with a Task

Start Here

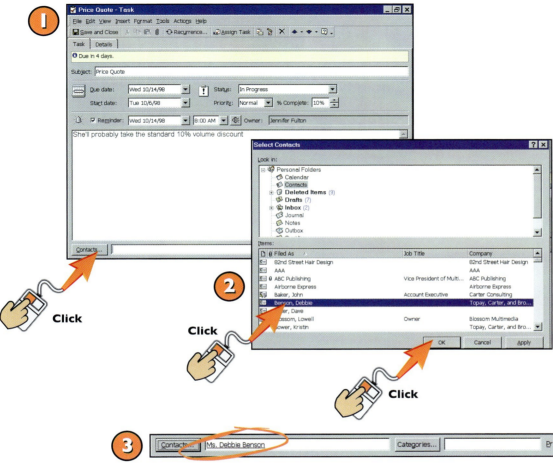

Click

Click

Click

If the task you're adding is for a client or a colleague, you may want to associate it with a contact name. Doing so allows you to easily track what you're doing (especially if that work is billable to a client).

① Click the **Contacts** button.

② Select the contact you wish to associate with this task, and click **OK**.

③ The name you selected appears in the **Contacts** box.

✅ **Looking Up a Contact's Information**
To look up contact information associated with a task, open the task by double-clicking it. Then double-click the contact name at the bottom of the task window.

✅ **Easy Association**
To create a new task and associate it with a contact at the same time, drag the contact's name onto the **Tasks icon** in the *Outlook bar*.

End Task

Page 145

Task 4: Adding a Recurring Task

Some tasks reoccur at regular intervals. For example, you might need to complete a project report every two weeks, pick up your daughter after soccer practice every Tuesday, or prepare performance reviews every quarter. Recurring tasks can be easily scheduled to reappear in the Calendar, without having to copy them from one day to another manually.

Start Here

Click

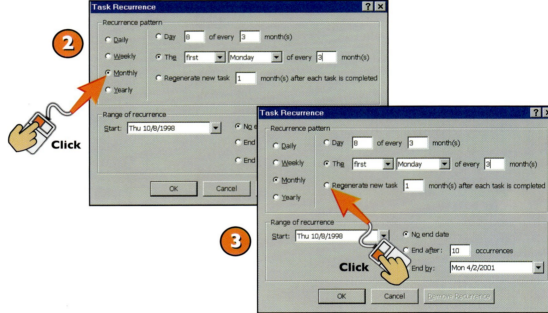
Click

Click

In the task window, click **Recurrence.**

Select a recurrence pattern, such as **Monthly**.

Select from the additional options that appear.

Next Step

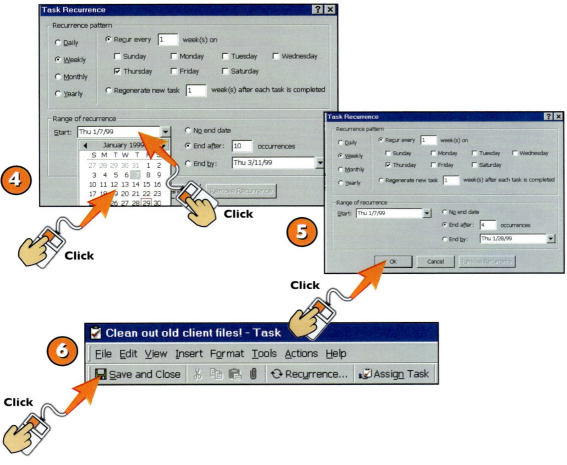

④ Select a start date for the recurrence in the **Range of recurrence** area.

⑤ Select a limit to the recurrence and click **OK**.

⑥ Click **Save and Close**.

Task 5: Updating the Status of a Task

If you want, you can periodically update the progress you're making on a particular task. You might want to do this if you need to update your boss (or someone else) on the progress you're making. You might also want to track your progress for your own peace of mind. In addition, keeping track of the number of hours you work on a task will help you when it comes time to bill your client (that is, if you bill by the hour).

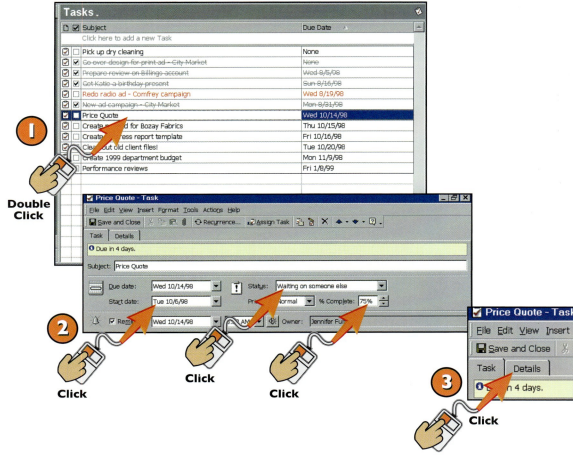

Start Here

Double Click

Click

Click

Click

Click

✅ Completing a Task

If the task is completed and you don't want to enter any of the details as shown here, you can quickly check it off your list by just clicking the check box in front of the task.

✅ Updating Your Boss on Your Progress

Once you update the status of the task, you may want to send a report to your boss. See Part 5, Task 6.

① Double-click the task you wish to update.

② Make changes to the **Start date**, **Status** and **% Complete** as needed.

③ Click the **Details** tab.

Next Step

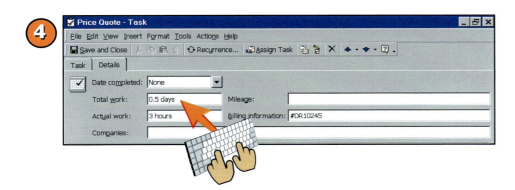

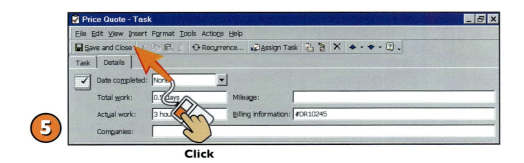

Click

4 Type the estimated and actual number of work hours. Enter other information as needed.

5 Click **Save and Close**.

 The Task That Wouldn't Die
Even after a task is completed, it is not removed from the Tasks list. This enables you to look up information related to an old task. If you want to remove the task from the list, see Part 7, Task 1 for help.

End Task

Task 6: Sending a Status Report

After updating the progress you've made on a particular task, you may want to share your good work with someone else, such as your boss or a client for whom you are working. When you send a status report to someone, it's sent in an *email message*.

Start Here

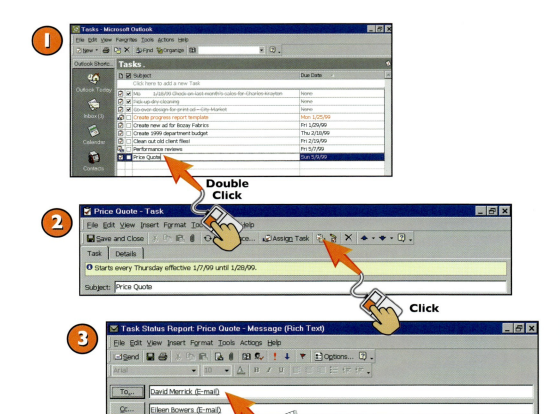

If this task was assigned to you, and then the person who assigned it was already set up to receive automatic updates—just click the **Details** tab and check the **Update** list area. If a name appears there, all you need to do for that person to receive a status report is to update the status of the task. See Part 5, Task 5 for help.

1 Double-click the task about which you'd like to send a status report.

2 In the Task window, click **Send Status Report.**

3 Type or select the address of the person(s) to whom you wish to send the report.

Next Step

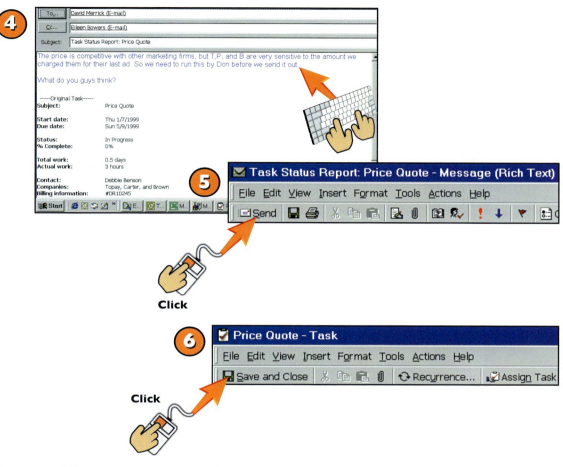

Click

Click

4 Type any additional comments in the large text box.

5 Click **Send**.

6 Click **Save and Close**.

If you want, you can reassign a task to someone else, such as a subordinate, an assistant, or a colleague. When you reassign a task, you lose ownership of it, which means that you can no longer make any changes to it. If the task is accepted by the person to whom you wish to assign it, he or she becomes the owner, and only he or she can make changes. You can, however, ask to receive automatic updates, so you can keep abreast of his or her progress on the task.

> ⓘ **WARNING!**
> When you assign a task to someone, you are making a request. That person has the option to decline the task, in which case, its ownership is returned to you.

> ⓘ **WARNING!**
> Although you can assign a task to multiple people, you cannot receive automatic status reports if you do.

Task 7: Assigning a Task to Someone Else

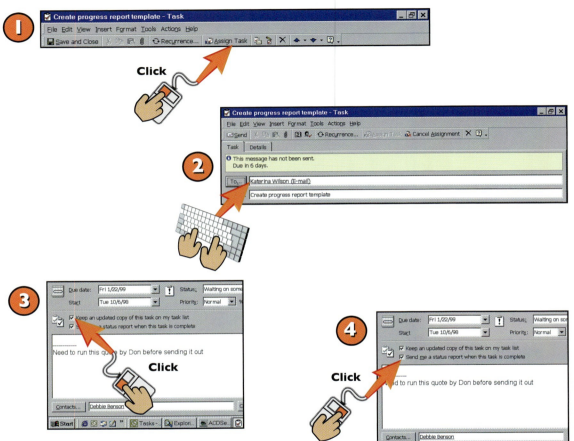

1 In the Task window, click **Assign Task.**

2 Type or select the address of the person(s) to whom you wish to assign the task.

3 Select **Keep an updated copy of this task on my task list** if you wish to receive automatic updates.

4 Select **Send me a status report when the task is complete** if you also want a report when the task is finished.

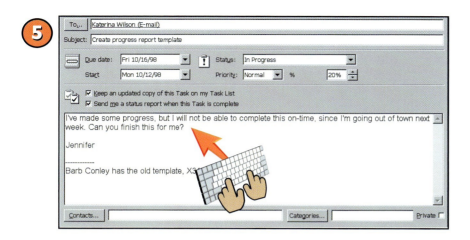

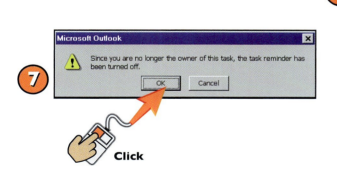

Type your message in the notes area.

Click **Send**.

If there was a reminder set for the task, you'll see a warning. Click **OK**.

End Task

WARNING!
Unless the person to whom you wish to assign this task is connected to you through a *network*, he or she will receive an ordinary email, minus the Accept/Decline buttons. The task will not be automatically placed on their Tasks list, and you will not be able to receive automatic updates.

Task 8: Responding to a Task Request

When someone attempts to assign a task to you, the request comes in the form of an email message. You can accept, decline, or even reassign the task to someone else. However, until you decide what to do, the task is temporarily assigned to you—meaning that you own it and are the only person who can make changes to the task. So it's important that you accept, decline, or reassign the task as soon as possible.

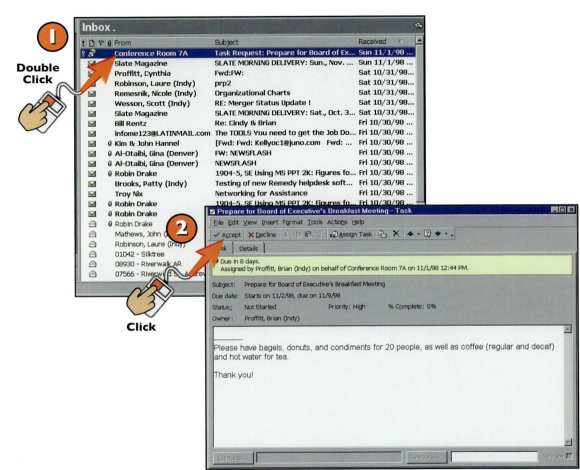

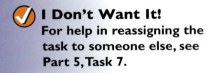

✓ I Don't Want It!
For help in reassigning the task to someone else, see Part 5, Task 7.

1 Double-click the **task request**.

2 Click **Accept** or **Decline**.

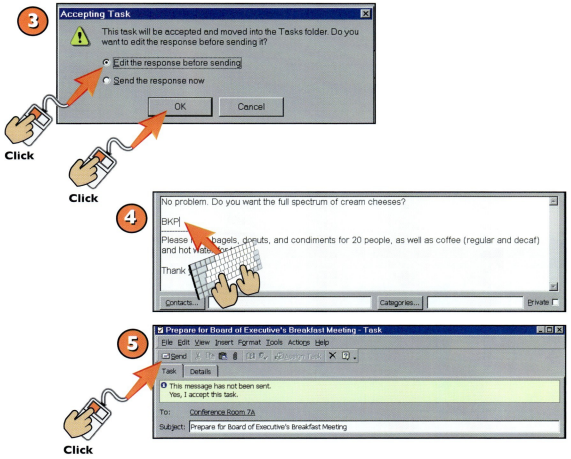

If you accept a task, it's placed in your Tasks list automatically. As you update your progress on the task, the person who assigned it to you can receive automatic updates, or you can send updates yourself manually (see Part 5, Task 6). If you decline a task, it's returned to the person who sent it.

3 Click **Edit the response before sending** and click **OK**.

4 Type your response in the notes area.

5 Click **Send**.

Task 9: Sharing Your Tasks List

In earlier tasks, you learned how to share your *Inbox*, Calendar, and *Contacts* list with others in your organization. If you want, you can allow others to view your Tasks list and the progress you're making on specific tasks. You can also grant higher levels of access if you want, such as allowing certain members of your department to make additions, changes, and deletions to the Tasks list on your behalf.

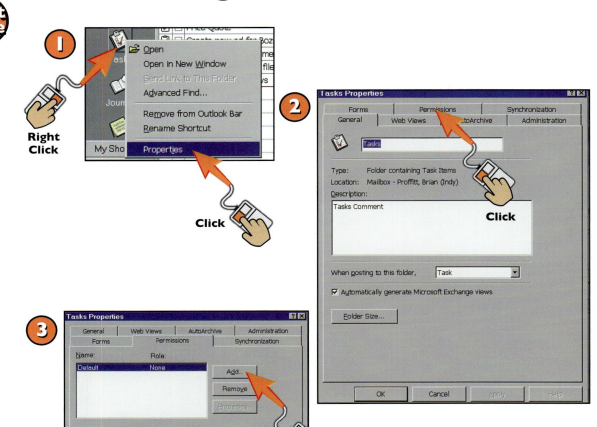

⚠ WARNING
Your company must use Microsoft Exchange Server as its email server for you to perform this task.

✓ Make Someone Your Assistant
If you want to grant someone *permission* to view, create, change, and delete items in your Tasks list, select **Editor** from the **Roles** list in step 6.

① Right-click the **Tasks** folder and select **Properties**.

② Click the **Permissions** tab.

③ Click **Add**.

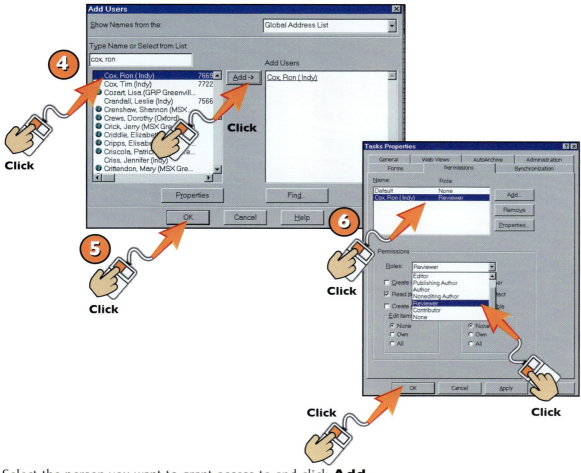

4 Select the person you want to grant access to and click **Add**.

5 Click **OK**.

6 Select the person in the **Name** list, select **Reviewer** from the **Roles** list, and click **OK**.

✅ **Internet Access**
You can also grant access to your Tasks list through the *Internet* (or a company *intranet*). See Part 7, Task 8 for more information.

End Task

Task 10: Adding a Task While Giving a PowerPoint Presentation

With PowerPoint, you can create a series of slides and present them onscreen in front of a large audience. During your presentation, a question may come up that requires some type of follow-up action. You don't need to jot the task down and try to remember to add it to your things to do; instead, you can add the task directly to the Tasks list so you won't forget it.

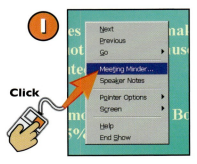

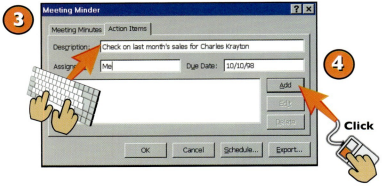

1 Right-click any slide during the presentation and select **Meeting Minder**.

2 Click the **Action Items** tab.

3 Type a **Description** for the task, who you want to assign it to, and a **Due Date**.

4 Click **Add**. Repeat steps 3 and 4 to add additional tasks.

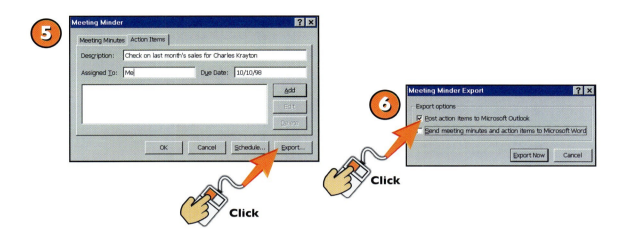

Reassign a Task
Tasks generated by the Meeting Minder are posted to your Tasks list, but you can easily reassign the tasks when needed. See Part 5, Task 7 for help.

Can I Get a Copy of That?
If you want to print out your action items (tasks) and your *meeting* minutes, you can select that option in step 6 and print them out using Microsoft Word.

5 Click **Export**.

6 Select **Post action items to Microsoft Outlook.**

7 Click **Export Now**.

8 Click **OK** to return to the presentation.

Task 11: Printing The Tasks List

If you find yourself out of the office often, you can print out your Tasks list so it is always close at hand. And, if you happen to use a day planner, you'll be glad to know that you can easily adjust the paper size and paper type of the printout so that it will be able to fit.

Click

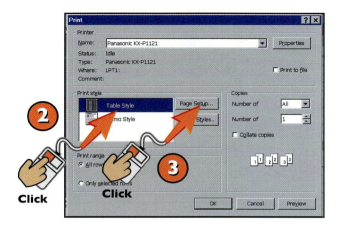

Click   Click

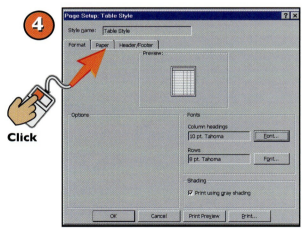

Click

✅ **To Select or Not to Select?**
When you select Table style (which prints only what's displayed onscreen), all tasks are printed unless you select the ones you want. If you choose Memo style (which prints all data related to a task), *only* the selected tasks are printed. To select the tasks you want, press **Ctrl** and click each task. To select all tasks, press **Ctrl+A**.

✅ **Your Point of View**
Additional print style options may appear in the Print dialog box depending on the view you are using.

1 Open the **File** menu and select **Print**.

2 Click the **Print style** you want and select the options you desire from the **Print range** area.

3 Click **Page Setup**.

4 Click the **Paper** tab.

Next Step

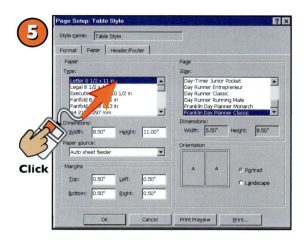

Click

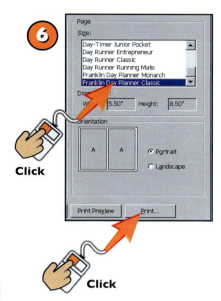

Click

Click

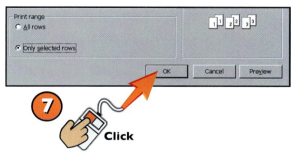

Click

⑤ Select a paper size from the **Paper Type** list.

⑥ Select a layout from the **Page Size** list and click **Print**.

⑦ Click **OK** to print your Task list.

✓ Preview it Before Printing

You may want to click **Print Preview** in step 6 to preview the Tasks list before you print it. That way, you can easily return to the Page Setup dialog box and make any necessary changes.

✓ The Quickest Way to Print

Once you've made selections in the Page Setup dialog box to fit your day planner, just click the **Print** button the next time you want to print your Tasks list.

PART 6

Maintaining a Journal and Keeping Track of Small Notes

Items that you create within Outlook can be tracked in the **Journal**. For example, you can track all the **email** messages and **faxes** that you send or receive from a particular client. So you don't clutter the Journal with information you don't need, you can specify which contacts (and which activities) you want the Journal to track.

Outlook also can track the work that you do with Microsoft Office. Want to know when you last updated the budget worksheet in Excel? Check the Journal. Want to see if you wrote that letter to Mr. Billings? Check the Journal. Since certain activities are recorded for you automatically, maintaining your Journal is easy. However, you can add your own entries to the Journal when you need to. For example, you might want to record the minutes of a **meeting** or a conversation you had with a client over lunch.

Instead of constantly misplacing important bits of information you used to jot down on whatever was handy, such as a bit of paper or a sticky note, why not record them in the Notes section of Outlook? In Notes, you can record quick thoughts, directions to a client's office, small reminders, questions you want to remember to ask, and other items. And, you'll always know where you can find that important piece of information. Notes appear onscreen looking like paper sticky notes. However, you can also display the notes (and their contents) in a long text list.

Tasks

Task 1: Automatically Recording Your Activities

Outlook tracks certain tasks automatically (email-related activities such as incoming and outgoing messages, *meeting requests* and responses, and *task requests* and responses). In addition, *if you tell it to,* Outlook can also track activity related to the documents you create with Microsoft Office—such as letters, memos, and reports created with Microsoft Word, worksheets created with Excel, databases maintained in Access, and presentations created with PowerPoint.

⚠ WARNING!
The activities you selected will be recorded *from now on.* To record previous activities, you must enter them into the Journal manually. See Part 6, Task 5 for help.

✓ Stop Recording
To stop recording Office activities, just repeat the steps here.

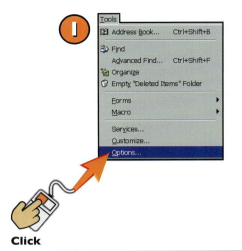

Click

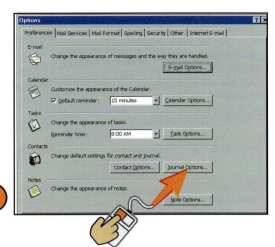

Click

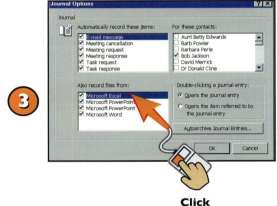

Click

1 Open the **Tools** menu and select **Options**.

2 Click **Journal Options**.

3 Click the Microsoft Office programs whose activities you want automatically recorded in the **Also record files from** list.

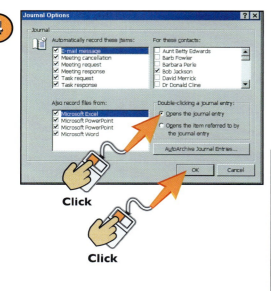

Click

Click

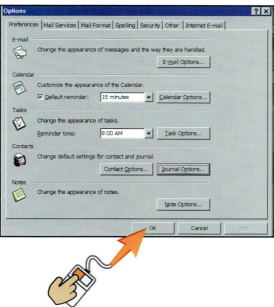

Click

At the top of the Journal Options dialog box, you can track certain activities related to a particular client, by selecting that client and then choosing the activities you want to track (such as email messages). This activity is already tracked for you automatically, for every contact, in the *Contacts* folder. If you make a selection here, the activity will be recorded in the Journal as well. You might want to do this if you want to be able to view activities related to key clients quickly.

④ Click the option that describes what you want to happen when you double-click a Journal entry. Click **OK**.

⑤ Click **OK** again.

✓ **Viewing Office Activities**
Once you start tracking them, activities related to your Office documents are recorded in the Journal. To view them, see **Part 6, Task 2** for help.

End Task

Task 2: Viewing Journal Activities

Normally, Journal entries are sorted by type (such as email messages, or meeting requests). However, you can view Journal entries by contact and by company, among other options. Selecting the view that best suits your needs allows you to locate the entries you want to review quickly. You can choose the view you want to use by opening the **View** menu, selecting **Current View**, and making a selection.

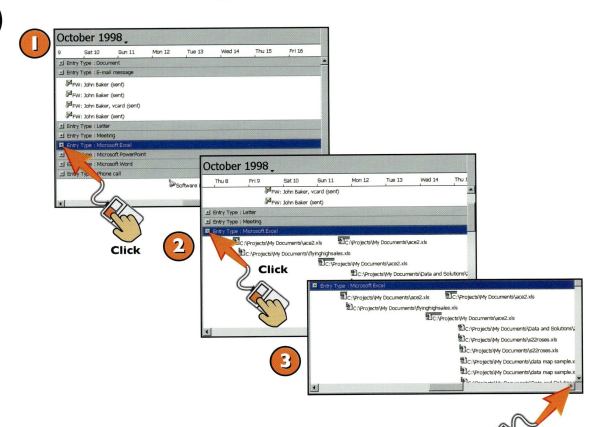

Click

Click

Click

✔ **Which Contacts are Recorded?**
Contacts whose activities you've chosen to record in the Journal are proceeded in the Contacts list by a special icon that includes a small pencil. For help recording activities for particular contacts, see Part 6, Task 1.

1 To display the items in a **group**, click its **plus sign**.

2 To hide them again, click the **minus sign** that appears.

3 To view entries that are not currently displayed, use the scroll bars.

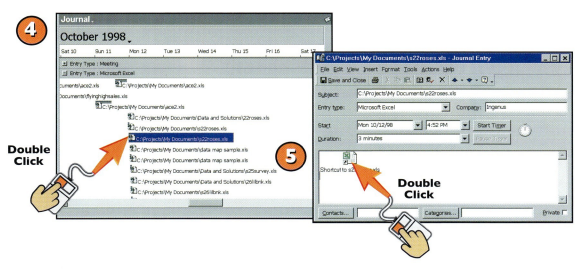

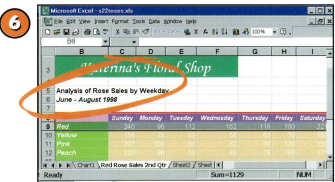

4 Double-click any entry to view its contents.

5 Double-click the **shortcut** icon to open the **document** or Outlook item.

6 The document or Outlook item is displayed.

✓ **View Contact Activities**
Some activities are recorded automatically and stored in the **Contacts** folder. Other activities are stored there because you *link* them to a contact name when you create them. See Part 6, Task 3 for help viewing activities stored in the **Contacts** folder.

End Task

Task 3: Viewing Entries Stored in the Contacts Folder

Some activities are recorded automatically and stored in the Contacts folder. These activities are all email related: incoming and outgoing messages, meeting requests and responses, and task requests and responses. Other activities are stored in the Contacts folder because you link them to a contact name when you create them. Once an activity is linked to a contact, it can be viewed from within the Contacts folder.

Start Here

Double Click

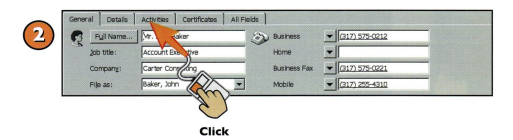

Click

✓ **Keeping Tabs on Important People**
If you've got a couple of key clients that you like to keep tabs on, you might find it convenient to record their activity in the Journal as well. That way, you can quickly review activity for all your key clients in one convenient spot. See Part 6, Tasks 1, 2, and 5 for more information.

① Double-click the contact whose activities you wish to view.

② Click the **Activities** tab.

Next Step

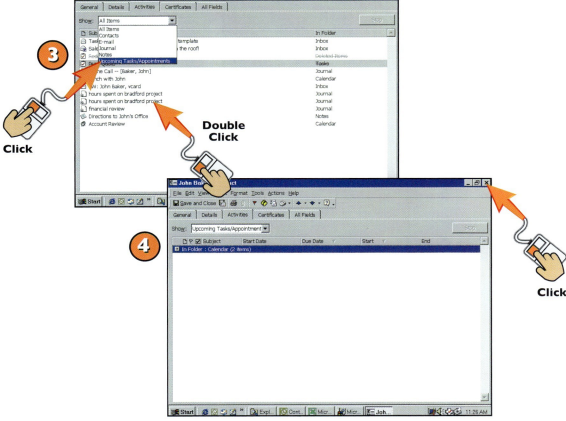

Click

Double Click

Click

3 Select the type of activity you wish to view. Double-click an activity to view its details.

4 When you're through viewing the entry, click the **Close** button.

If you talk to a lot of people throughout the day, you know how important it is to make a note of the conversation so you don't forget what it was that you talked about. Unfortunately, one of the activities that the Journal can not automatically track is an incoming phone call. (For help recording an outgoing call to a contact, see Part 4, Task 6.)

Task 4: Creating a Journal Entry for an Incoming Phone Call

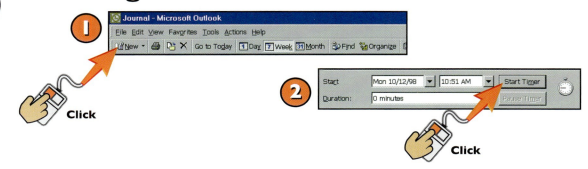

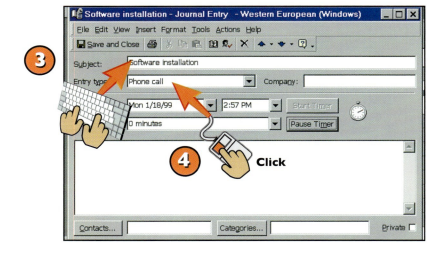

✅ **Call From a Contact**
If the phone call is from someone in your Contacts list, drag his or her name onto the **Journal icon** on the *Outlook bar* to quickly create your entry.

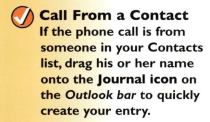

1 Click the **New Journal Entry** button.

2 Click **Start Timer**.

3 Type a description for the call in the **Subject** box.

4 If needed, select **Phone call** from the **Entry type** box.

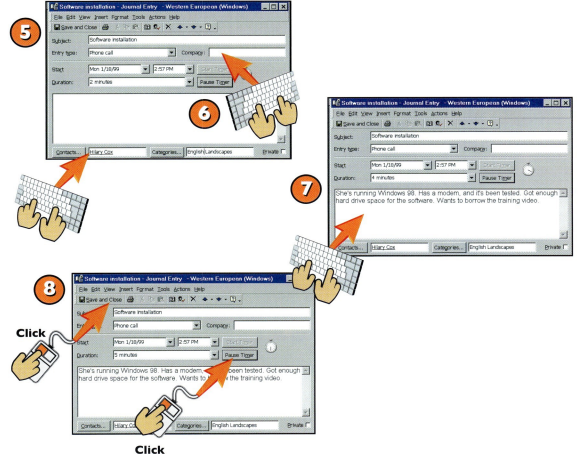

You can easily enter the information you want to remember manually. Once entered into the Journal, you can review the notes of your phone call easily—see **Part 6, Task 2.** If you associate a contact with the phone call in step 5, the phone call is also saved to the Contacts folder. See **Part 6, Task 3** for help in viewing it there.

Click

Click

⑤ Type the name of the person who's calling in the **Contacts** text box.

⑥ Type a **Company** name if applicable.

⑦ Enter your notes in the large text box.

⑧ When you're through, click **Pause Timer**. Then click **Save and Close**.

✓ **Other Entries Too!**
If you want to manually record other types of entries in the Journal, such as a conversation, a non-Office file, or an Outlook item not associated with a contact, see **Part 6, Task 5** for help.

Task 5: Entering Activities Manually

Although Outlook tracks a lot of activities for you automatically, there are a many activities that it does not track such as files not created with Microsoft Office and **appointments, tasks, or notes.**

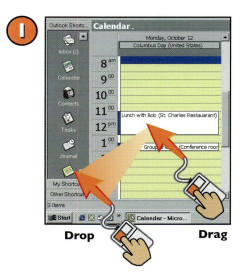

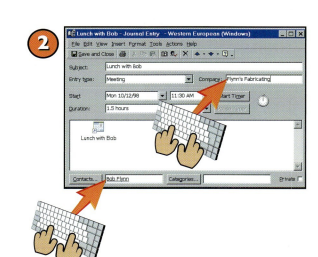

Drop   Drag

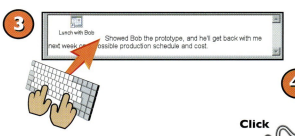

Click

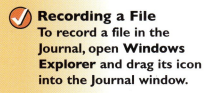

✓ **Recording a File**
To record a file in the Journal, open **Windows Explorer** and drag its icon into the Journal window.

✓ **Recording a Conversation**
To record a face-to-face conversation in the Journal, follow the same steps listed in Part 6, Task 4, but select **Conversation** from the **Entry type** drop-down list.

① Drag the item you wish to record, and drop it onto the **Journal icon** in the Outlook bar.

② Type or select the name of the person related to this activity in the **Contacts** text box. Type a **Company** name if applicable.

③ Enter your notes in the large text box.

④ Click **Save and Close**.

Task 6: Creating a Note

Start Here

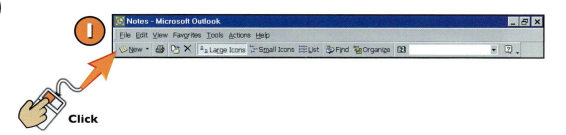

Click

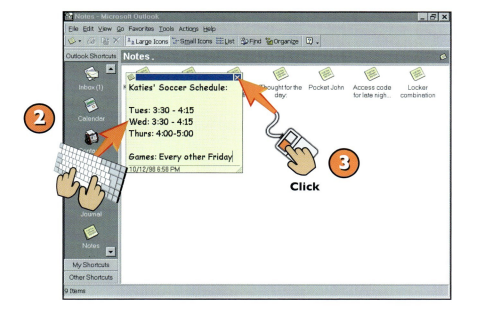

Click

Notes are the electronic equivalent of sticky notes. In Notes, you can jot down questions or answers you don't want to forget, important directions, things to remember, a classy quote, or any small bit of information you deem important. **By adding your notes to Outlook, you won't run the risk of misplacing them. Also, you can organize them easily.**

✓ **Quick Creation**
You can also create a note by dragging an Outlook item onto the **Notes icon** on the Outlook bar. If you drag a contact name onto the Notes icon, the note will also appear on the Activities tab of that contact.

✓ **Making a Change**
To change a note later, double-click it, make your change, and then close it again. The changes are saved automatically.

1 Click the **New Note** button.

2 Type your note into the window. You can copy text from a file with the **Edit**, **Copy** and **Edit**, and **Paste** commands.

3 Click the note's **Close** button.

Task 7: Colorizing Your Notes

Start
Here

Outlook lets you organize your notes with color. For example, you might make all the notes related to a particular client blue. For another client, you might choose green. For another, yellow. The choice is yours. Using colors effectively can help you quickly identify the note you want to view.

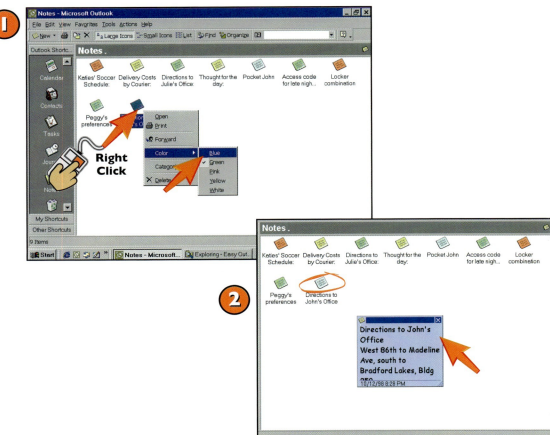

Default Color
By default, a new note is yellow in color. To change the default, open the **Tools** menu, select **Options**, and then click **Note Options**. Select what you want from the **Color** drop-down list, and then click **OK**.

Arranging Your Notes
To arrange your notes by their color, open the **Current View** menu and select **By Color**.

1 Right-click the note you want to change, select **Color,** and then click the color you want.

2 The icon for the note and the note itself is displayed in the color you choose.

End
Task

Task 8: Printing a Note

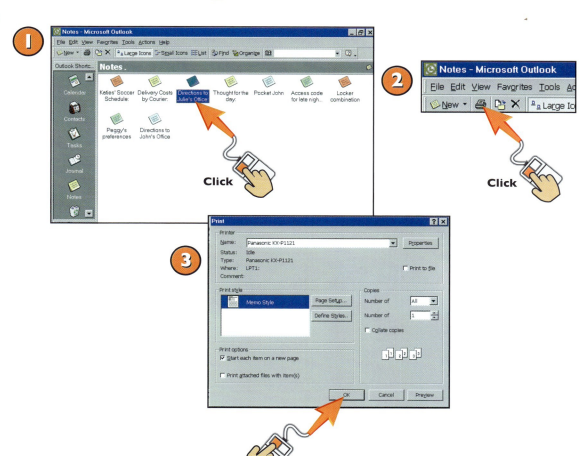

Click the note you want to print.

Click the **Print** button.

Click OK.

As you learned in **Part 6, Task 6**, it's easy to create a note. Well, it's even easier to print them out so you can take them with you. For example, if one of your notes contains directions to a client's office, you can print it out so it would be easy to reference on the drive over.

1. Click the note you want to print.

2. Click the **Print** button.

3. Click **OK**.

✓ **Print Them All!**
To print all your notes, select them all by pressing **Ctrl+A**. Then click **Print** and click **OK**.

Deleting, Organizing, and Locating Your Outlook Items

The objects you create using Outlook are called items. An Outlook item, therefore, might be an **email message**, an **appointment**, a **meeting**, a **contact**, a **task**, a journal entry, or a note.

The procedures for working with all Outlook items are the same, regardless of what that item is. For example, to delete an old email message, you follow the same steps that you would to delete an appointment. Since the procedures for managing your Outlook items are the same, they are presented together in this part for easy reference.

Tasks

Task 1: Deleting an Item

When items are no longer needed, you can delete them from Outlook. Deleted items are not actually removed; instead they are moved to the *Deleted Items* folder. This allows you the chance to retrieve an accidentally deleted item. From time to time, you'll want to empty this *folder* to permanently delete your unused items (see Part 7, Task 2 for help).

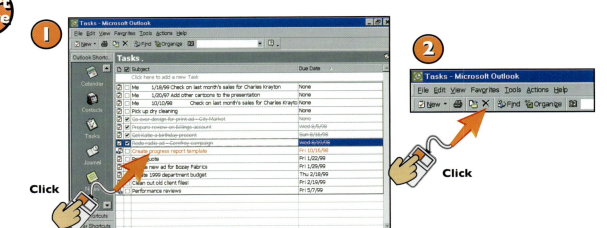

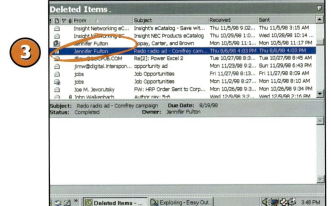

✔ **Delete Multiple Items**
To select multiple items for deletion, press **Ctrl** as you click each one.

① Click the item you want to delete.

② Click **Delete**.

③ The item is moved to the Deleted Items folder.

Task 2: Emptying the Deleted Items Folder

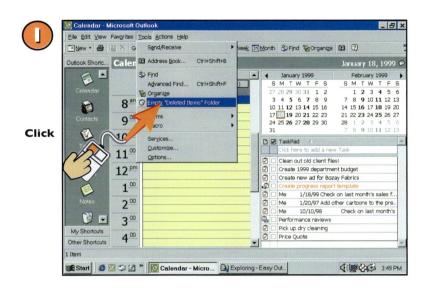

Click

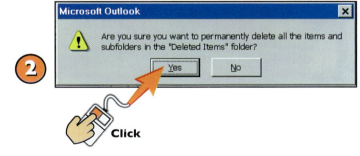

Click

When you delete an item, it's not really removed from Outlook; instead, it's simply moved to the Deleted Items folder. Thus, the Deleted Items folder acts as a "holding area" for old items, providing a second chance for items you may delete accidentally. To permanently remove your deleted items, you must empty the Deleted Items folder.

WARNING!
To retrieve an accidentally deleted item *before* itís removed from the Deleted Items folder, right-click it and select **Move to Folder**. Select the folder where you want the item placed, and click **OK**.

Automatic Trash Service
You can have Outlook automatically empty the Deleted Items folder every time you exit the program. Just open the **Tools** menu and select **Options**. Click the **Other** tab, and then select the **Empty the Deleted Items folder upon exiting** option.

① From any Outlook folder, open the **Tools** menu and select **Empty "Deleted Items" Folder**.

② Click **Yes**.

If you're on a company *network* that uses *shared folders* (Outlook folders to which you and others have access), you may occasionally find an interesting message, note, *event*, contact, or task that you want to copy to your own Outlook folders. Or you might want to copy one of your own items into someone else's *Calendar*, *Tasks* list, *Inbox*, or *Contacts* list to which you have access. Or, perhaps you want to reorganize your own items by creating new folders and copying selected items into them. In any case, it's easy to copy an item into another folder.

✅ Copy That

If you want to make a copy of an item to create a new item that's similar, use the **Edit, Copy** and **Edit, Paste** commands. To create a copy of a contact, use the **Actions, New Contact from Same Company** command.

Task 3: Copying an Item

Start Here

Click

Click

Click

Click

1 Press **Ctrl** and click the item(s) you want to copy.

2 Open the **Edit** menu and click **Copy to Folder**.

3 Click the folder to which you want to copy or move the selected item(s). (If needed, click the **plus** sign in front of a folder to display its subfolders. To create a new folder, click **New**.)

End Task

Task 4: Moving an Item

Start Here

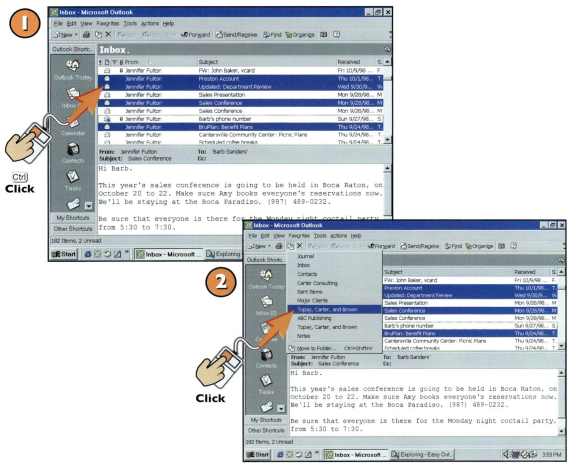

After using Outlook for a while, it's easy to collect a lot of items, especially email messages. Some items you'll want to delete, but others you'll want to organize. One way to make sure you can locate like items quickly is to move them into their own folders.

✔ New Folders

If the folder to which you want to move the items does not yet exist, you can create it and move selected items into it in one simple series of steps. See Part 7, Task 6 for help.

⚠ WARNING!

If you've created a lot of similarly named subfolders of major folders in the Inbox, Contacts, and so on, (see the second figure), you might want to select **Move to Folder** in step 2 and use the dialog box to select the folder you want to use.

1 Press **Ctrl** as you click the items you wish to move.

2 Click **Move to Folder**, and select the folder to which you want to move the items.

Task 5: Searching for a Particular Item

You might waste a lot of time trying to locate a particular email message, appointment, meeting, contact, *Journal* entry, note, or task. But Outlook has an easier way to find what you need, using the Find Items command. Once an item is found, you can open it, copy it, move it, delete it, print it—in short, you can do anything you need to do.

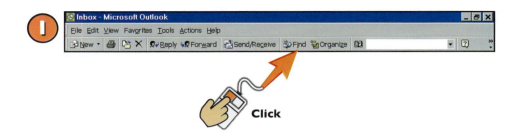

Click

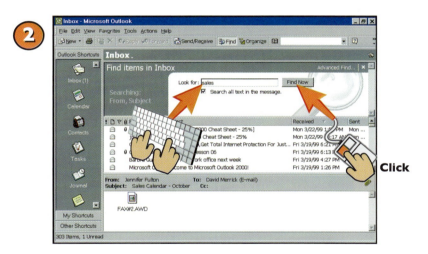

Click

WARNING!

If you can't find the item you're looking for, you may need to enter more precise criteria. Click **Advanced Find** and enter the criteria you want to use.

Click **Find**.

Type the word(s) you are looking for, and click **Find Now**.

Next Step

Click

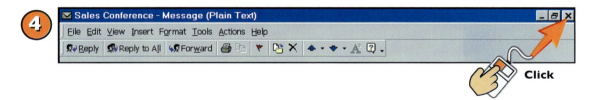

Click

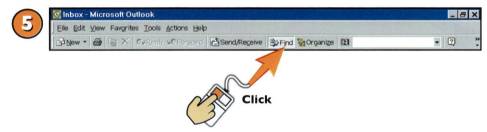

Click

③ A list of items matching your criteria appears. Double-click an item to view it.

④ After viewing the item's contents, click its **Close** button.

⑤ When you're through viewing the found items, click **Find** to remove the listing.

On the hard drive, you use folders to organize your files. In Outlook, you can use folders for this same purpose: to organize your Outlook items. When you create a folder, you can place it within whatever folder you want. For example, you might create several folders in the Inbox folder to organize your email messages. After creating a new folder, you can easily move items into it. (If you need help moving items into an existing folder, see Part 7, Task 4.)

✓ **Managing Your New Folder**

The **File, Folder** menu contains commands that you can use to remove a folder later, to copy or move it, or to delete it.

⚠ **WARNING!**

If you perform these steps in the Inbox folder, an additional option appears allowing you to set up *rules* for managing your mail. This option is explained in Part 2, Task 35.

Task 6: Creating Folders to Organize Items

Start Here

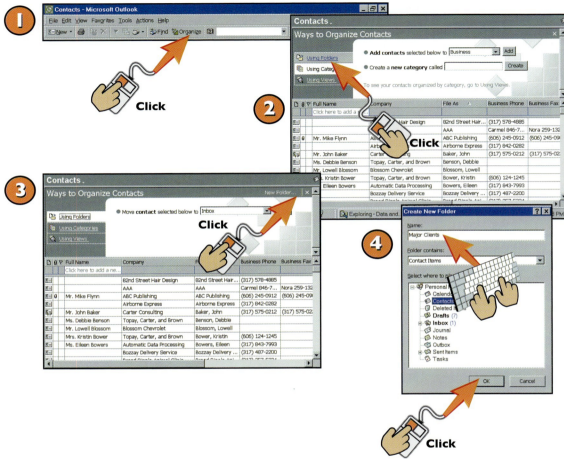

① Click **Organize**.

② Click **Using Folders.**

③ Click **New Folder.**

④ Type a **Name** for the folder.

Next Step

5

6

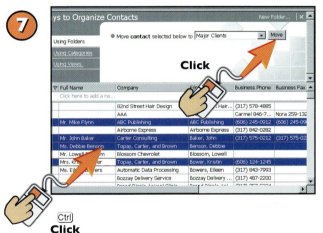

7

Click

Ctrl
Click

8

Click

5 Select the folder where you want this folder placed, and click **OK**.

6 Click **Yes** to create a shortcut to this folder in the Outlook Bar.

7 Press **Ctrl** and click each item you wish to move into the new folder, and then click **Move**.

8 Click **Organize** to remove the Ways to Organize Contacts box.

✔ **Where's the Folder?**
If you create a *shortcut* to your new folder in step 6, you can display its contents by clicking the **My Shortcuts** button on the *Outlook bar*, and then clicking the icon for the new folder. If you did not create a shortcut, open the **Folder List** and select the folder from there. (See Part 1, Task 1 for more information.)

When you assign categories to your items, you can use these categories to help you identify items of a particular type. For example, you might want to add the *category* "Peterson Project" and use it to identify items related to that particular project. Or you might want to separate all your personal contacts from your business ones—and you can, simply by selecting the proper category for each contact and then grouping the items in that folder by category.

Categories can be assigned when you create an item now or later. In this task, you'll learn how to assign a category to several items at once and how to create new categories (if needed).

⚠ **WARNING!**
You can't organize email messages by categories.

Task 7: Using Categories to Organize Items

① Press **Ctrl** and click the items you wish to categorize.

② Click **Organize**.

③ Select the category you want to assign to the selected items from the drop-down list.

Next Step

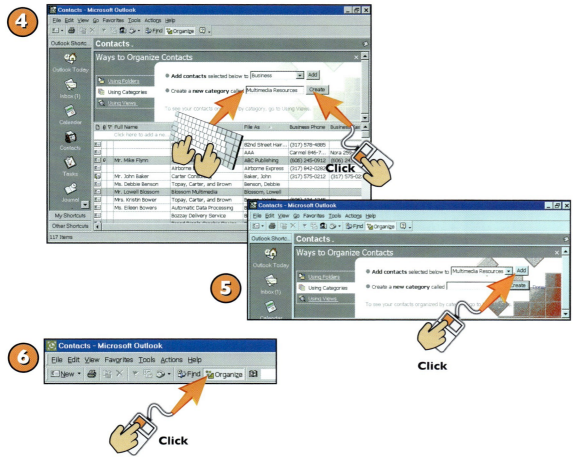

Click

Click

Click

(4) If you don't see a category you like, type a name for the new category and click **Create.**

(5) Click **Add** to add the selected items to the selected category.

(6) Click **Organize** to remove the Ways to Organize box.

✓ **Multiple Categories**
You can assign multiple categories to the selected items by repeating steps 3 to 5.

✓ **Display by Category**
To display your items by category, click the **Using Views** tab and click **By Category.** If the Ways to Organize box is not displayed, you can open the **View** menu, select **Current View,** and select **By Category** instead.

Task 8: Archiving Important Items

Cleaning Out the Junk

When an item is archived, it's saved in a special folder on your hard drive and deleted from Outlook. Think of archiving as a process that clears out old junk from within Outlook. But unlike deleting old items (which removes them permanently), if you need to, you can always retrieve items from the *archive* later (see Part 7, Tasks 9 and 10).

✓ **Folder Only Control**
To turn *AutoArchive* off for a folder, click the **Clean out items older than XX option** in step 3 to remove the check mark.

✓ **Turning It Off Completely**
To turn AutoArchive off completely, open the **Tools** menu, select **Options**, and click the **Other** tab. Click **AutoArchive**, and turn off the **AutoArchive every XX** option.

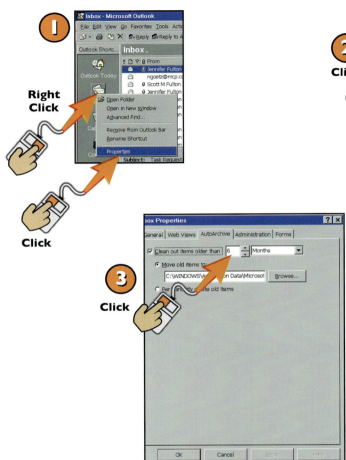

Start Here

Right Click

Click

Click

Click

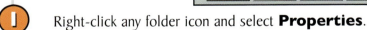

① Right-click any folder icon and select **Properties**.

② Click the **AutoArchive** tab.

③ Select the age at which items are archived.

Next Step

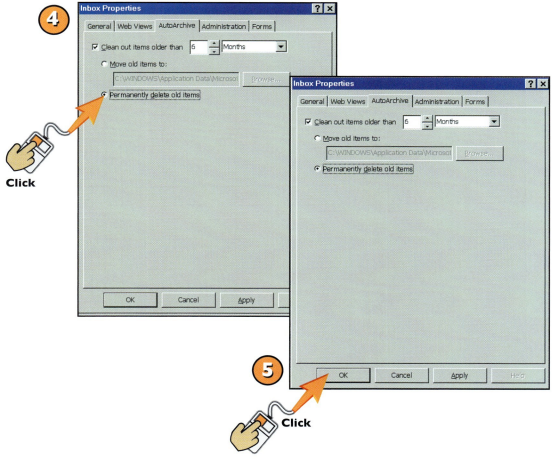

Click

Click

By default, AutoArchive occurs every two weeks, archiving items in the Inbox, Calendar, Tasks list, and Journal that are older than 6 months. Items in the *Sent Items* and Deleted Items folders that are older than 2 months are also automatically archived, although you can turn AutoArchive on for other folders, such as **Notes** or folders you may have created yourself. You can also turn off the AutoArchive feature for any folder or tell it to permanently delete items and not archive them.

4 To delete rather than archive items, click **Permanently delete old items**.

5 Click **OK**.

Task 9: Retrieving Archived Items

Archived items are saved in a special file from which you can later retrieve them when needed. When items are retrieved, they are copied from the archive file back into their original folder. You can select how you want duplicates handled—for example, if an archive file exists for an item already in the folder, do you want the older file to overwrite the existing file? Or would you prefer to let both files co-exist? You can also choose to simply not import any duplicate files. The choice is yours.

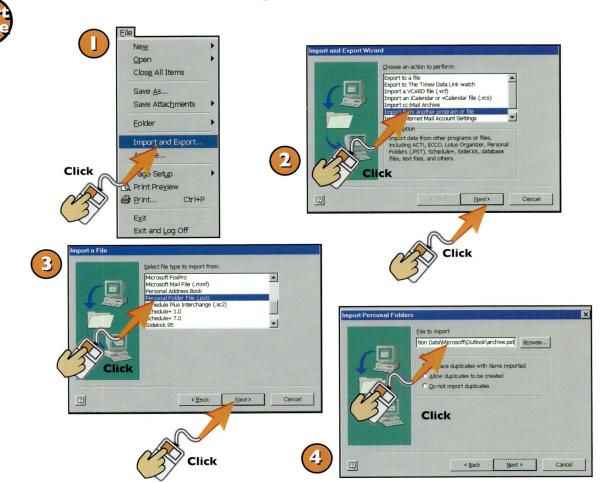

✓ Retrieving Selected Items

In this task, you'll learn how to retrieve all the archived items in a particular folder. In Part 7, Task 10, you'll learn how to retrieve selected items from an archive.

1 Open the **File** menu and select **Import and Export**.

2 Click **Import from another program or file**. Click **Next>**.

3 Click **Personal Folder File (.pst)**. Click **Next>**.

4 Type the path of the file you want to import in the **File to Import** text box.

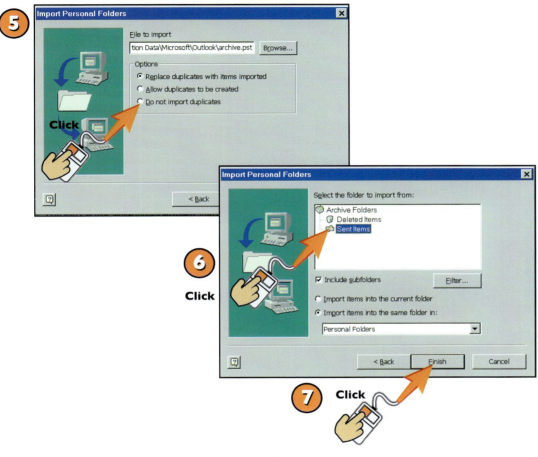

5 Select how you want duplicates handled. Click **Next>**.

6 Click the folder whose items you wish to import.

7 Click **Finish**.

Archiving Files
For help in archiving files (removing older files from Outlook), see Part 7, Task 8.

End Task

Getting Back Selected Items

In Part 7, Task 9, you learned how to retrieve all the archived items from a folder and return them to Outlook. Here, you'll learn how to be a bit more selective about which items you retrieve. For example, perhaps you've just discovered that you need to review an old email message that's been archived, but you don't want to retrieve all of your archived messages.

✅ **Archive First!**
For help in archiving files (removing older files from Outlook), see Part 7, Task 8.

Task 10: Opening the Archive File to Retrieve Selected Items

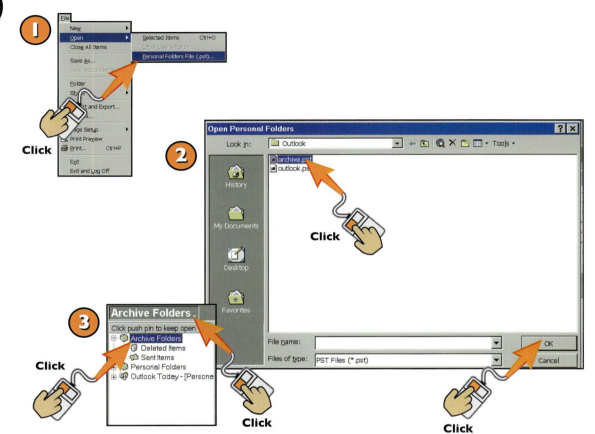

1 Open the **File** menu, select **Open,** and then select **Personal Folders File (pst)**.

2 Click the file you wish to open and click **OK**.

3 Click the **Folder List** and select an archived folder.

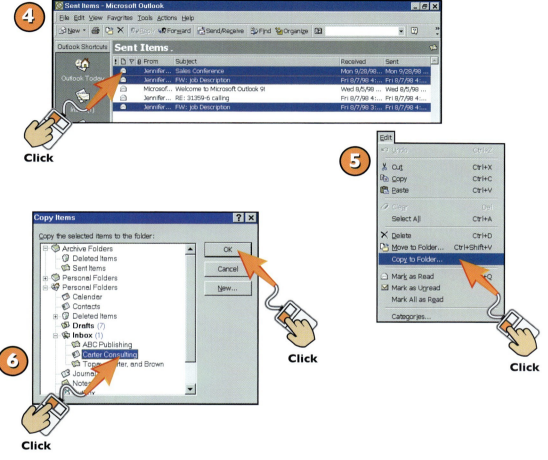

Click

Click

Click

Click

✓ **Close the Archive**
After retrieving the selected files, you can close the archive by changing to the archive folder first. Then right-click the heading **Archive Folders** at the top of the window and select "**Close Archive Folders.**"

④ Press **Ctrl** and click the items you want to retrieve.

⑤ Open the **Edit** menu and select **Copy to Folder**.

⑥ Click the folder into which you want the items copied. Click **OK**.

End Task

Creating Your Own Groups of Icons

To help you locate the folders you want to use, you can add your own group of icons to the Outlook bar. For example, if you have created your own folders, you may want to create a separate group with icons that point to them. Or, if you have access to other people's folders, you might want a separate *group* for them.

✔ **Add a Shortcut**
After you create your new group, you'll want to add some icons (shortcuts) to it (see Part 7, Task 12 for help).

✔ **Getting Rid of a Group**
To remove a group later (and its shortcut icons), right-click the group and click **Remove Group**.

Task 11: Adding a New Group to the Outlook Bar

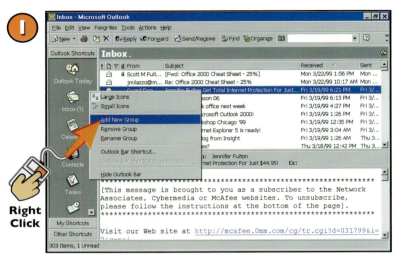

Right Click

Right-click the Outlook bar and select **Add New Group**.

Type a name for the new group and press **Enter**.

Click

Outlook's Built-in Groups

When Outlook is first installed, it's Outlook bar is divided into three groups: **Outlook Shortcuts, My Shortcuts, and Other Shortcuts.** The Outlook Shortcuts group is the one with which you're probably the most familiar: it contains **Outlook Today,** **Inbox, Contacts,** and so on. **My Shortcuts** contains icons for the **Drafts, Outbox,** and **Sent Items** folders. The **Other Shortcuts** group provides quick access to **My Computer, My Documents,** and **Favorites.**

3 The new group appears on the Outlook bar.

4 To display the items for this group, click its button on the Outlook bar.

5 After items have been placed in the group (as you'll learn to do in the next task) you can use them to display the contents of your favorite folders.

Task 12: Adding a Shortcut to the Outlook Bar

The groups on the Outlook bar help you organize your folders (or at least, the shortcut icons that point to them). If you have folders on the hard drive or the network that you use often, you can access their contents more quickly if you create a shortcut to them. You can also add shortcuts to the Outlook folders you've created (that is, if you didn't opt to have the shortcut created for you automatically when you created the folder).

Start Here

Right Click

Click

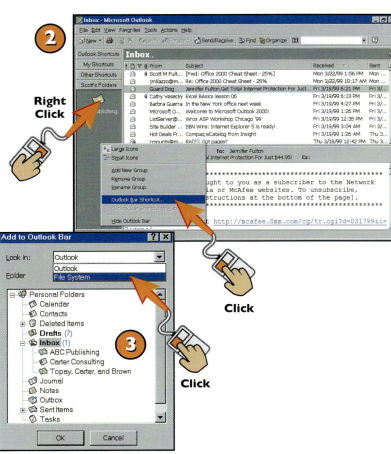

Click

Click

✔ **Create a Group**
If you'd like to create your own group on the Outlook bar, see Part 7, Task 11 for help.

✔ **Getting Rid of an Icon**
To remove an icon, right-click it and click **Remove from Outlook bar**.

1 Change to the group to which you want to add the new shortcut icon.

2 Right-click the Outlook bar and select **Outlook Bar Shortcut**.

3 Select the location of the folder from the **Look in** list.

Next Step

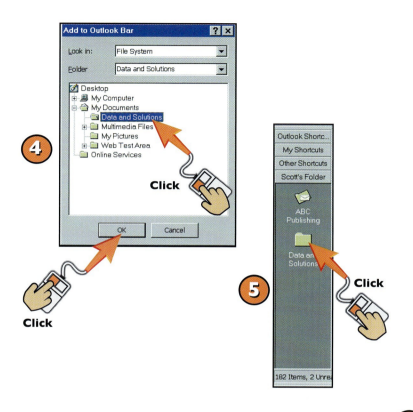

Click

Click

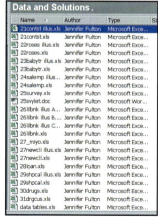

Click

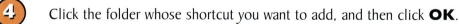
Click the folder whose shortcut you want to add, and then click **OK**.

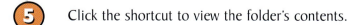
Click the shortcut to view the folder's contents.

The contents of the folder are displayed.

Using Net Folders, you can share Outlook items with others over the Internet. After publishing an Outlook folder as a Net Folder, you add or change items in it, and these items are sent over the Internet (as e-mail messages) to the people you list as subscribers.

Task 13: Sharing an Outlook Folder Over the Internet

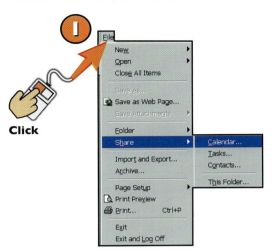

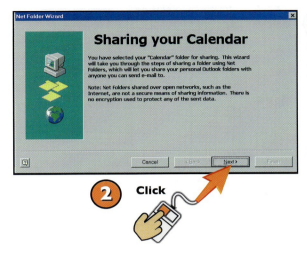

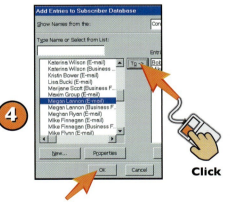

✓ **Accept or Decline**
After you publish your folder, an e-mail message is sent to each subscriber, who can either accept or decline the subscription. If they accept, updates to the file are sent via e-mail at the frequency you select.

1 Click **File**, click **Share**, then select the folder you want to publish.

2 If asked, click Yes to install this feature. Click **Next>**.

3 Click **Add.**

4 Select a person with whom you want to share this folder and click **To**. Repeat to add additional names, then click **OK**.

Next Step

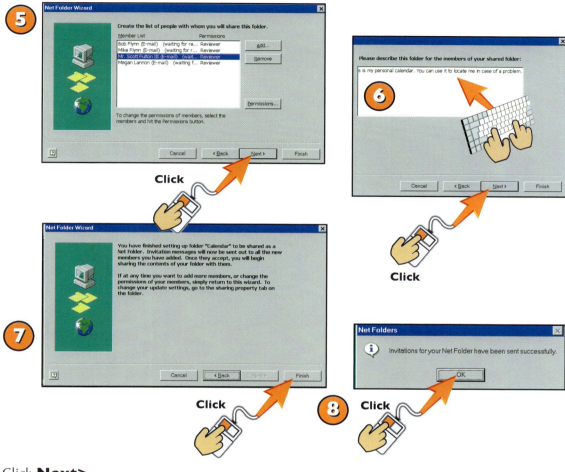

Normally, subscribers can only view items in a Net Folder, but you can grant higher permission levels to the folder to allow subscribers to add items, make changes, and delete items. Just select a subscriber in step 5, click **Permissions**, then select the level of permission you wish to assign and click **OK** to return to the Net Folder Wizard.

5   Click **Next>**.

6   Type a description of the folder and click **Next>**.

7   Click **Finish**.

8   Click **OK**.

Using the Office Assistant to Get Help

The Office Assistant (in this case, a paper clip named Clippit) appears the first time you start Outlook, and after that, whenever he senses that you could use some help. Don't let Clippit's childlike appearance fool you, behind him is Outlook's very powerful help system.

New to Outlook 2000 is HTML Help. This help system is more powerful than before, and because of its similarity to Web browsing, it's a lot easier to use.

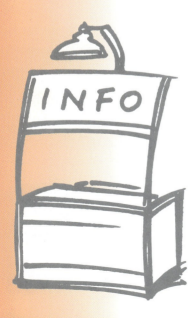

Tasks

When you're working in Outlook and you have a question, just ask the Office Assistant. Simply call up the assistant, type your question (such as "How do I schedule a meeting?") or a few keywords (such as "schedule meeting"). The assistant responds with a listing of possible Help topics from which you can choose. Each topic provides details and steps for completing a particular procedure.

WARNING!
If the assistant is already onscreen, but the Help bubble into which you type questions is not, just click the assistant to display the bubble.

WARNING!
If none of the topics in step 3 describe what you want, click the See More… option at the bottom of the list to view more suggestions. To return to the first list, click the See previous option.

Task 1: Asking the Assistant a Question

Start Here

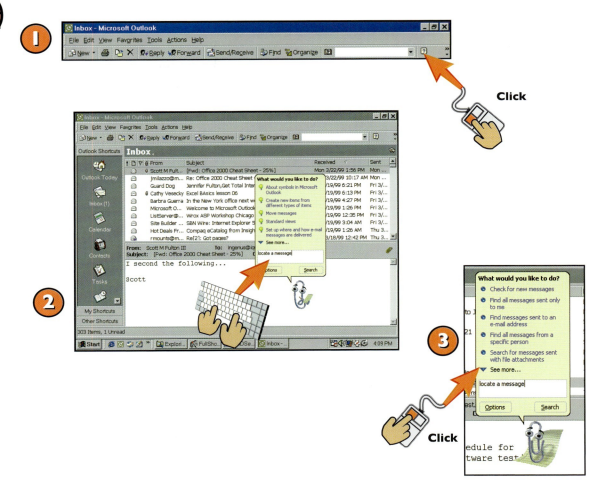

Click

1 Click the **Microsoft Outlook Help button** or press **F1** to display the assistant.

2 Type a question or some keywords into the text box and press **Enter**.

3 Click the topic that best describes what you're trying to do.

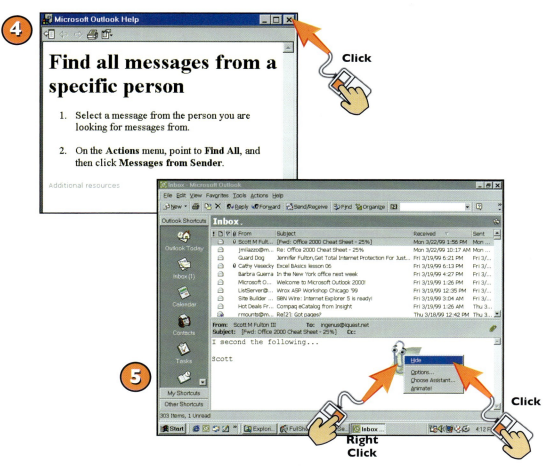

After selecting a topic from the **Office Assistant bubble**, a Help window appears. Click an underlined word to see its definition, or to jump to a related Help page. Click **>>** to jump to another Help screen. You can return to a previous Help topic by clicking **Back** as many times as you need. Return to where you were by clicking **Forward**. To display tabs for the **Contents** and the **Index** that enable you to look up a topic yourself, click **Show**.

4 When you're through reading the topic, remove the Help window by clicking its **Close** button.

5 If you want to remove the assistant as well, right-click him and select **Hide**.

✓ **Searching the Web**
If you still can't locate a topic you want, you can click the **None of the above, look for more help on the Web** option in the topics list. This allows you to send your question to Microsoft's technical support.

Clippit is not the only Office Assistant you can use. There's Mother Nature (a spinning globe), Office Logo, The Genius (an Einstein look-a-like), F1 (a robot), Links (a cat), and Rocky (a dog). So if you find Clippit's antics annoying, just change to one of the other assistants.

Task 2: Selecting a New Assistant

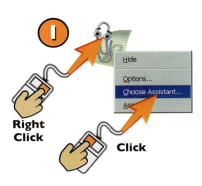

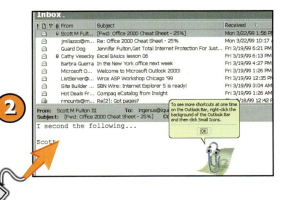

Right Click

Click

Click

Click

WARNING!
You may need the Outlook 2000 CD-ROM to install your new assistant.

1 Right-click the Office Assistant and select **Choose Assistant**.

2 Click **Back** or **Next** to display another assistant. Continue as needed.

3 When you find an assistant you like, click **OK**.

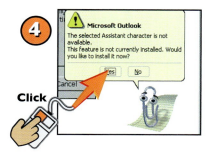

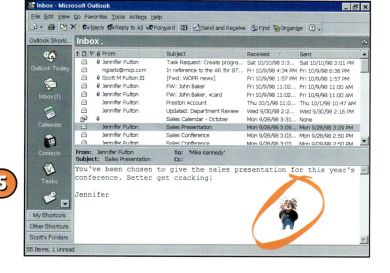

 If you see a message telling you that the assistant you want to use is not installed and asking if you want to install it, click **Yes**.

 The assistant you selected is displayed.

Task 3: Displaying a Hint

As long as the Office Assistant is active, it keeps watch over the way you work. If you take the long way around, as it were, to complete some task, the Office Assistant displays a light bulb to indicate that he has a suggestion to complete the task you just performed more quickly.

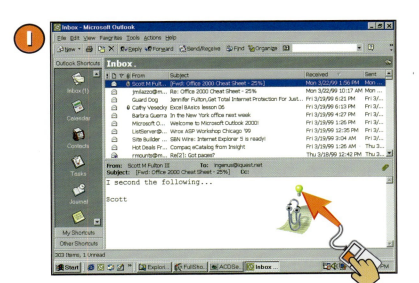

Click

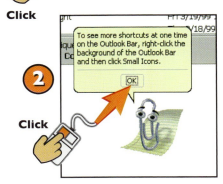

Click

✓ **Controlling the Number of Hints**
You can control the type of hints that the Office Assistant displays with the Options dialog box. See Part 8, Task 4 for help.

① Click the light bulb over the Office Assistant.

② Click **OK** when you're through reading the hint.

Task 4: Setting Options for the Assistant

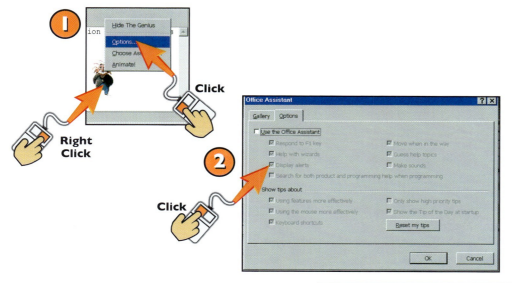

Click

Right Click

Click

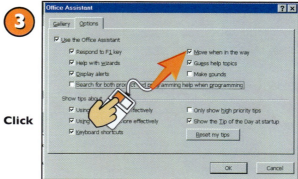

Click

When you click the **Microsoft Help** button or press **F1**, the Office Assistant appears. You type a few keywords into his bubble and press Enter, and a list of topics appears. You select one of these topics, and a help window appears. If you'd rather bypass this process and display the Help dialog box immediately, you can, with the help of the Office Assistant Options dialog box.

✔ **Other Options as Well**
If you want to use the Office Assistant, you can still customize him. For example, you can control his sound, the type of alerts and tips he displays, and even the initial display of topics.

! **WARNING!**
There is only one Office Assistant. So be aware that if you make changes to his appearance or behavior while in Outlook, that will affect him even when you switch to other Office programs such as **Word** or Excel.

① Right-click the assistant and select **Options**.

② To turn the assistant off completely, click the **Use the Office Assistant** option to remove its check mark.

③ If you decide to use the Office Assistant, you can customize him by turning on or off the options you want and then clicking **OK**.

Installing Outlook 2000

Choosing Between Internet Only and Corporate/Workgroup Email Service

Prior to installing Outlook 2000, you need to make a decision as to which software to install:

- *Internet only*—Choose this option if you use a dial-up Internet email service *only*. If you also want to send and receive faxes or use some third-party email service such as America Online, you must choose the Corporate or Workgroup option.

- *Corporate or Workgroup*—Choose this option if you send and receive email through your company network (whether you also send and receive Internet mail), or if you want to use America Online, Prodigy, CompuServe or some other third-party email service. This option also allows you to use the Microsoft Exchange Server to share Outlook folders and to use Microsoft Fax to send and receive faxes.

- *No Email*—Choose this option if you want to use Outlook to organize your appointments, meetings, events, and tasks, but you do not intend to use it to send and receive email.

Installing Outlook 2000

To install Outlook 2000, follow these steps:

1. After installing Office 2000, double-click the **Microsoft Outlook** icon on the Windows desktop to begin.

2. The Outlook 2000 Setup screen is displayed. Click **Next>**.

3. If an older version of Outlook already exists on your computer, you'll be asked if you're currently using it. Select the program you are currently using to enable Outlook 2000 to import your old settings or choose none of the above. Click **Next>.**

4. Select the email service option (Internet Only, Corporate or Workgroup, or No Email) that you wish to use. Click **Next>.**

5. The Outlook 2000 window appears. To maximize it, double-click the title bar.

6. If you were using an older version of Outlook previously, you'll be asked if you want to make Outlook 2000 the default manager for your contacts. Click **Yes**.

7. The Office Assistant appears, offering help. You can choose to review the options that are new (useful if you're upgrading from an older version of Outlook), to learn more about using the Office Assistant, or to simply start using Outlook. Click your choice to begin.

Installing Add-ins

Outlook comes with many add-ins, or mini programs that perform a particular function. For example, you might want to install the Microsoft Fax add-in to send and receive faxes. The process is the same for all the add-ins, so you can follow these steps to install any one you might need. Here are the steps for adding the Microsoft Fax add-in:

1. Open the **Tools** menu and select **Options**.

2. Click the **Other** tab.

3. Click **Advanced Options**.

4. Click **Add-In Manager**.

5. Click **Install**.

6. Select the add-in you want to install, and click **Open**. To install Microsoft Fax, select the file, **awfext.ecf**.

7. The add-in you selected is installed. Click **OK** three times until you are back to Outlook.

8. To begin using the add-in, you must restart Outlook. Open the **File** menu, and select **Exit**.

9. Double-click the Microsoft Outlook icon on the Windows desktop to restart Outlook.

Adding an Information Service

An information service provides Outlook with the capability of managing a specific information source. For example, an information service called Outlook Address Book was set up for you automatically to manage your contact information. You could set up the information service, Personal Address Book, to manage a subset of your contacts list, such as major clients only or personal contacts only. Another information service, Public Folders, was established to manage your various Outlook folders.

The most important information service that you need to establish is your Internet email service (assuming of course, that you want to send and receive email through the

Internet). To set up this service, you must gather the following information from your Internet Service Provider (ISP):

- The name of your POP3 or IMAP server (incoming mail server) and its port number.

- The name of your SMTP server (outgoing mail server) and its port number. You'll also need to know whether or not this server requires authentication and possibly a different password and logon name.

- Your logon name and password.

- Your email address.

Follow these steps to set up your Internet email information service:

1. Open the **Tools** menu, and select **Services**.

2. Click **Add**.

3. Select **Internet E-Mail** and click **OK**.

4. Click the **General** tab.

   - Type a name for the service in the text box provided.

   - Type your **Name**.

   - Type the name of your company under **Organization**.

   - Type your **Email address.** For example: `jfulton@indy.net`.

- Type the address to which you want replies to your messages to be sent, if different than your normal email address.

5. Click the **Servers** tab.

   - Type the address of your SMTP server. For example: `smtp.indy.net.`

   - Type the address of your POP3 server. For xample: `pop3.indy.net.`

   - Type your logon name and password.

   - If your SMTP server requires additional authentication, select that option, and click **Settings** to enter the logon name and password.

   ✅ **Bypass the Password**
   If you don't want to type in the password each time you check for mail, make sure that the option Remember password is *not checked*.

6. Click the **Connection** tab.

   - Select the type of connection you use.

   - If you're using a dial-up connection and you've already created the Dial-Up Networking file under Windows, select it from the drop-down list. If not, click **Add** to create one.

⚠️ **WARNING!**
You'll need additional information from your ISP to create a Dial-Up Networking file, such as the phone number you dial into, the TCP/IP settings, and whether or not you need a dial-up script. Your ISP will provide you with specific step-by-step instructions for creating your Dial-Up Networking icon.

7. The settings on the **Advanced** tab do not typically need to be changed, so don't change anything unless you've been specifically instructed by your server administrator to do so.

8. When you're through, click **OK**.

Setting Up Word as Your Email Editor

Outlook allows you to use Microsoft Word as your email editor, provided you have it installed, of course. If you decide to use Word, you'll gain its rich set of tools to help you create your email messages. Specifically:

- Word's Format toolbar helps you add formatting such as fonts, bold, italic, or underline, bulleted or numbered lists, and tables to your email messages. You can even highlight text using the highlighter.

- Spell Checker helps you verify that your messages are error free as you type. You don't have to remember to check them yourself. In addition, AutoCorrect even corrects common typing errors as they occur.

- Additional email templates (stationary) help you create a professional or fun look to your email messages.

- Web addresses and email addresses are automatically converted to links for you. The recipient of your message needs only to click these links to use them.

- Document Map helps you review your email messages quickly by displaying the "threads" that connect original messages to replies.

If you decide you want to use Word as your email editor, follow these steps:

1. Open the **Tools** menu, and select **Options**.

2. Click the **Mail Format** tab.

3. Select the option, **Use Microsoft Word to edit email messages**.

4. Click **OK**.

Address Book   The folder that contains your Contacts information.

appointment   A meeting that involves you and someone outside your organization. See also *meeting, event*.

archive   A special file that contains older Outlook items, such as old email messages, that have been removed from your Outlook folders. You can retrieve items from the archive when needed. See also *AutoArchive*.

attachment   A file or an Outlook item that is sent with an email message. You can also attach a file or item to other Outlook items as well, such as a contact, an appointment, or a task.

AutoArchive   An option that automatically removes older Outlook items from your system, placing them in a file where they can be retrieved when needed. See also *archive*.

AutoPreview   A view used in the Inbox in which a short summary of each message's contents is displayed just following the message header.

AutoSignature   A text file that can be displayed at the end of email messages you send. For example, you might create a signature file that contains your name, title, company, phone number, email address, and other information you want to include in every message.

balloon   The message box in which you can type questions to the Office Assistant.

BCC   See *blind carbon copy*.

blind carbon copy   A copy of a message that's sent to someone in secret; the other recipients of the message will not see this person's name (or email address) in the message header. See also *carbon copy*.

browser   See *Web browser*.

Calendar   One of Outlook's main folders in which your appointments, meetings, and events are kept.

carbon copy   A copy of a message that's sent to someone. Unlike a blind carbon copy, all recipients of the message will see this person's name and email address in the message header. See also *blind carbon copy*.

category   A method of organizing your Outlook items. For example, when creating a new item such as a contact, you can select the categories to which it applies (such as personal) and then sort the entire Contacts list by category.

CC   See *carbon copy*.

Contacts   One of the main Outlook folders. The Contacts list contains all of your business and personal contacts and their addresses, phone numbers, email addresses, and other information.

conversation   See *thread*.

Date Navigator   Use the Navigator to change from one date to another in Calendar. You can also select multiple dates to display by simply pressing **Ctrl** and clicking them.

delegate   A person to whom you grant access to one or more of your Outlook folders. See also *permission*.

Deleted Items   When you delete an item from an Outlook folder, it is not actually removed, but simply moved to this folder. To delete items permanently, you must empty this folder.

distribution list   A list containing multiple email addresses. You can use a distribution list to send the same email to many people quickly.

document   An item created with an Office application, such as Word, Excel, or PowerPoint. You can create Office documents from within Outlook.

draft   An unfinished email message. When you save an email message without sending it, it's saved to the Drafts folder.

drag and drop   To drag and drop, you click an item, hold down the mouse button, and drag that item to where you want it to be. To drop it, release the mouse button. You might use drag-and-drop to create an new Outlook item using information from an existing item.

For example, you could drag an email message onto the Contacts icon in the Outlook bar to create a new contact entry.

email Short for electronic mail. Email is a message sent from one computer to another using a modem or a network connection.

event An all day occurrence, such as a birthday, conference, holiday, or anniversary. See also *appointment, meeting*.

fax Short for facsimile. A fax is one method for transmitting text and graphics over a telephone line by using a modem. Outlook can be set up to both send and receive faxes.

filter A method you can use to narrow (filter) a list display. For example, if you chose the view, "Last Seven Days" in the Inbox, Outlook would apply a filter to display only the messages received in the last seven days.

flag An icon that indicates a special item, such as an email message you want to follow up on.

folder Each folder contains a particular type of Outlook item, such as the Contacts list that contains all your contact information.

forward The process of sending a copy of a message you've received to someone else.

group A method you can use to organize the items in a list. For example, if you chose the view, "By Company" in the Contacts list, Outlook would group your contacts by company. To display all the items in a group, click its **plus** sign. To hide them again, click the **minus** sign that appears.

HTML Short for HyperText Markup Language, the language of the World Wide Web. If you use HTML to create your email messages, you can add text formatting such as graphical stationary, a special font, bold, italic, underline, text color, and so on. However, only people that use an email program that supports HTML formatting will be able to view such mail properly.

hyperlink A bit of underlined text that, when clicked, takes you to a page on the World Wide Web (or to another page in Outlook help).

importance A method of indicating the relative importance of an email message.

Inbox One of the main Outlook folders. Incoming email messages are placed in the Inbox. See also *Outbox, Sent Items*.

Information Viewer The area of the Outlook window in which items are displayed.

Internet A worldwide collection of interconnected networks. Outlook supports the use of the Internet for sending and receiving email messages. In addition, you can connect to Microsoft's Web site through your Internet connection when seeking additional help from within Outlook, or when looking up the location of a contact address.

Internet Explorer Microsoft's Web browser. See also *Navigator*.

Internet service provider A company that provides its client's with access to the Internet.

intranet A company-wide Internet-like network. See also *Internet*.

ISP See *Internet service provider*.

Journal One of the main Outlook folders. Here, you'll find links to Office documents you've created, along with email related activities, such as sending and receiving messages, meeting requests, and task requests. You can manually add more entries to the Journal as needed.

junk mail Unwanted and unsolicited email.

LAN

LAN   Short for local area network, a collection of interconnected computers limited to a small area, such as a single building.

link   To associate one Outlook item with another. For example, you might associate a task with a particular contact. This enables you to quickly view contact information while completing the task. It also enables you to track which tasks you've performed for particular contacts.

mail server   The computer that processes your email. Your mail server might be located on your company's network or, if you have a dial-up connection, on your ISP's computer.

meeting   An appointment that typically involves another person (or persons) within your organization. When you create a meeting, email invitations are automatically sent to everyone involved. See also *appointment, event*.

meeting request   A request to attend a meeting, sent in the form of an email. Voting buttons appear at the top of the window when the message is opened; to accept the meeting, click **Accept**, to decline, click **Decline**, and your response is automatically sent to the originator of the request. See also *voting buttons*.

message   See *email*.

modem   Short for modulator/demodulator. A modem converts digital data into sounds for transmission over a telephone line, where the data is converted back into digital form.

Navigator   Netscape's Web browser. See also *Internet Explorer*.

Net folder   An Outlook folder whose contents can be shared over the Internet or an intranet.

network   See *LAN*.

Outbox   An Outlook folder that contains messages that have not yet been sent. If you have a live connection to your email server (as opposed to a dial-up connection), messages may only spend a few seconds in the Outbox before they are sent.

Outlook bar   The bar of icons on the left side of the Outlook window. You access your Outlook folders by clicking these icons. In addition, you can add more icons to the Outlook bar to provide fast access to your private folders, for example.

Outlook Express   The email program that comes with Internet Explorer. Although it functions a bit differently, you can think of Outlook Express as a limited version of Outlook.

Outlook Today   A special folder in which a summary of today's (and the next few days) activities are displayed. You can quickly access unread messages, review today's appointments and meetings, and organize your tasks with the information on this page. Outlook can display this page at startup if you like.

permission   Provides access to your data for another user. See also *delegate*.

preview pane   The lower half of the Inbox window in which the contents of the selected message are displayed.

Public folder   An Outlook folder whose contents can be shared over a network that uses Microsoft Exchange server.

recipient   The person to whom an email message is sent.

recurring   A repeating item, such as a meeting that repeats at regular intervals such as weekly.

reminder   An alarm that warns you of an upcoming event, such as an appointment or task.

Remote Mail   A process that allows you to download selected email messages from your mail server.

Page 214

reply   A return message that's sent to a person who sent you a message. A reply typically contains the text of the original message, making it easy for the recipient to recall what he or she said.

resource   An item that must be managed and shared, such as a meeting room or an overhead projector.

right   See *permission*.

rule   Defines a set of actions to be taken when a particular event occurs. For example, you might set up a rule to define the folder in which you want particular incoming messages to be placed.

sender   The person who sent an email message.

Sent Items   Copies of the email messages you send are placed in this special folder.

service provider   See *Internet service provider*.

shared folder   A folder to which many people have access.

shortcut   An icon that is linked to a folder. You might add shortcuts to the Outlook bar to provide quick access to folders you use the most.

signature   See *AutoSignature*.

speed dial list   A list of people whose phone numbers you dial often. When you select a person from this list, Outlook will quickly dial the associated phone number for you.

stationary   Email messages that utilize a graphic or other colorful background through the use of HTML formatting.

status report   An email message that updates a colleague on the status of a task. See also *task*.

subject   A description of a message, task, appointment, meeting, or event.

task   An item that helps you keep track of something you need to do, such as completing a report, purchasing new equipment, or cleaning out your files.

TaskPad   A miniature version of the Tasks list that appears within the Calendar folder.

task request   A request to take on a task, sent in the form of an email. Voting buttons appear at the top of the window when the message is opened; to accept the task, click **Accept**, to decline, click **Decline**, and your response is automatically sent to the originator of the request. See also *voting buttons*.

Tasks   One of the main Outlook folders in which your "things to do" are kept.

thread   Related messages. The original message, along with any replies, form a thread, like the thread of a conversation, that can be followed at a later time by simply reading the messages in order.

URL   Short for Universal Resource Locator, the method used for assigning Internet addresses. Outlook allows you to enter an URL address to a Contact's Web page if you like.

vCard   A format for sharing contact information via the Internet.

voting buttons   Buttons that appear at the top of a message that allow you to return a message to the sender, containing your "vote," which corresponds to the voting button you click.

Web browser   A program that's used by Outlook to display a contact's Web information or to search for help on the Web. Popular Web browsers include Internet Explorer and Netscape Navigator. See also *Internet Explorer, Navigator*.

WWW   Short for World Wide Web, a part of the Internet that uses HTML to display text, graphics, sound, video, and so on.

Symbols

N

O

Notes

Notes

Notes

Notes

Notes

Notes

Get FREE books and more...when you register this book online for our Personal Bookshelf Program

http://register.quecorp.com/

 Register online and you can sign up for our *FREE Personal Bookshelf Program...*unlimited access to the electronic version of more than 200 complete computer books — immediately! That means you'll have 100,000 pages of valuable information onscreen, at your fingertips!

 Plus, you can access product support, including complimentary downloads, technical support files, book-focused links, companion Web sites, author sites, and more!

 And, don't miss out on the opportunity to sign up for a *FREE subscription to a weekly e-mail newsletter* to help you stay current with news, announcements, sample book chapters, and special events including sweepstakes, contests, and various product giveaways!

 We value your comments! Best of all, the entire registration process takes only a few minutes to complete...so go online and get the greatest value going—absolutely FREE!

Don't Miss Out On This Great Opportunity!

QUE® is a product of Macmillan Computer Publishing USA—for more information, please visit: *www.mcp.com*